Boxing
Cuba

Boxing Cuba

From Backyards to World Championship

Photographs by Katharina Alt

Herausgegeben von / Edited by
Michael Schleicher

Mit einem Vorwort von / With an introduction by
Charles Schumann

Mit Beiträgen von / With contributions by
Petra Giloy-Hirtz
Michael Schleicher
Claudia Strand

HIRMER   Museum
Fünf Kontinente

Inhalt   Contents

Cuba Libre

Als ich im Jahre 2003 in meiner Münchner Fotogalerie in der Maximilianstraße 36 unter dem Titel **ON BOXING** Schwarzweißfotografien aus Kuba von Alexander Pickl ausstellte, faszinierten mich diese Kinder ohne Schuhe und mit zerrissenen Hosen, die ihre ganze Hoffnung dem Boxsport anvertrauten. Sie spiegelten unsere Träume von Havanna, von einem einfachen und dennoch lebenswerten Leben mit karibischem Gefühl und Rhythmus, aber auch der harten Arbeit der Sportler. Und natürlich wünschten wir den legendären kubanischen Boxathleten weitere Welterfolge – ein Wunsch, den sie tatsächlich auch über die Jahre hinweg konstant bei Weltmeisterschaften und Olympischen Spielen einlösten.

Vielleicht ist gerade die Ausstellung **Boxing Cuba – From Backyards to World Championship** mit einzigartigen Fotoarbeiten von Katharina Alt ein wichtiger Mosaikstein zu dem großen Gesamtwerk aus Unabhängigkeit, Freiheit und Frieden für Kuba.

Ich bewundere die Kubaner für ihr Talent, unter so einfachen Bedingungen diese Welterfolge zu erzielen. Mein Traum ist es, einmal für zwei Woche nach Villa San Cristóbal de La Habana zu reisen und gemeinsam mit ihnen zu trainieren. Ich wünsche der Ausstellung und der von Michael Schleicher herausgegebenen Publikation viel Erfolg und natürlich allen kubanischen Boxkämpfern bei den XXXI. Olympischen Spielen in Rio de Janeiro unzählige Siege und einen reichen Medaillensegen.

Charles Schumann

In 2003, when I presented black-and-white photographs from Cuba by Alexander Pickl in an exhibition titled **ON BOXING** at my photo gallery at 36 Maximilianstrasse in Munich, I was fascinated by these barefoot kids with torn pants who put their entire hope in boxing. They reflected our dreams of Havana, of a life that is simple yet worth living, a life with a Caribbean feel and rhythm, yet also with the hard work of the athletes. And, of course, we wished the legendary Cuban boxers continued international success — a wish with which they, indeed, steadily complied at World Championships and Olympic Games over the years.

Perhaps the very exhibition **Boxing Cuba – From Backyards to World Championship** featuring unique photographic works by Katharina Alt will prove to be an important piece in the grand mosaic of independence, freedom and peace for Cuba.

It is due to their singular talent, their courage and stamina that they manage to be continually successful among the best of the world. My dream is to one day travel to Villa San Cristóbal de La Habana for two weeks and train with them. Much success to the exhibition and the publication edited by Michael Schleicher and, obviously, countless victories and medals galore for all Cuban boxers at the 2016 Olympic Games in Rio de Janeiro.

Charles Schumann

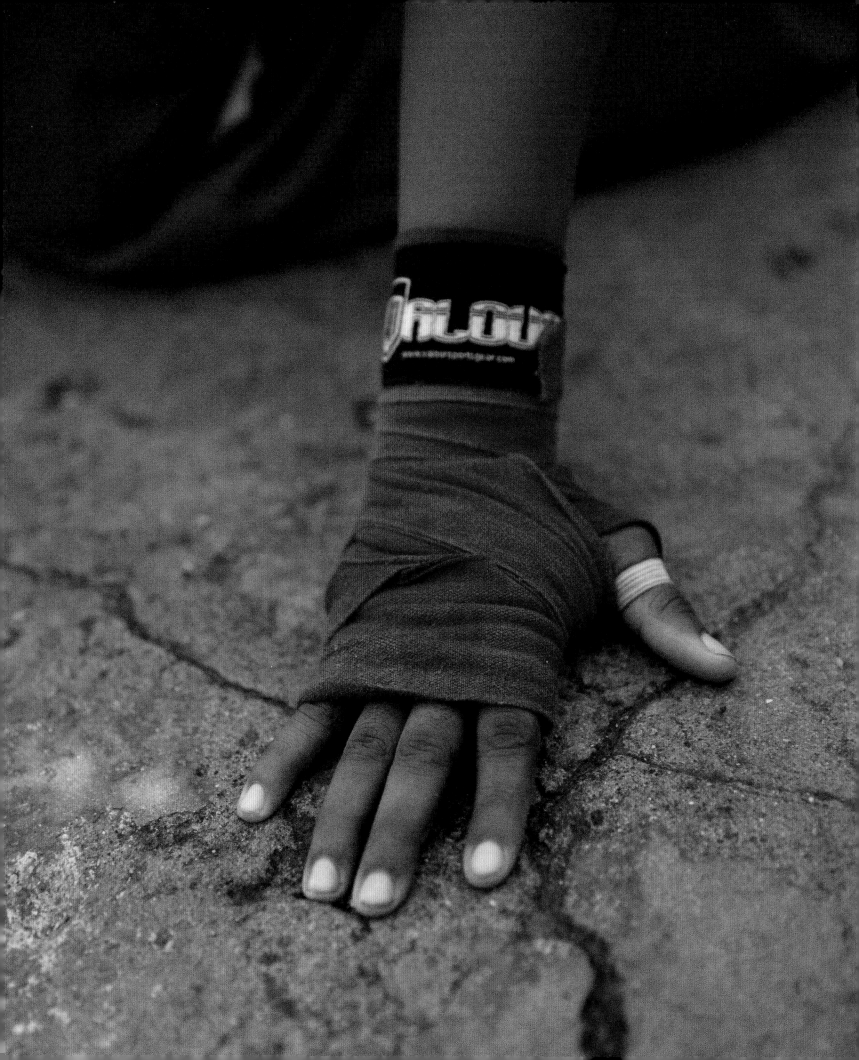

Jeder Boxkampf ist eine Geschichte –
ein einzigartiges und bis zum Äußersten verdichtetes Drama ohne Worte.
Joyce Carol Oates

Ich habe vor nichts Angst, habe ein gutes Herz und kann niemanden quälen;
ja, ich kann nicht einmal mit ansehen, dass jemand gequält wird.
Kid Chocolate

Each boxing match is a story,
a unique and highly condensed drama without words.
Joyce Carol Oates

I am not afraid of anything; I have a good heart and can't stand torturing anyone.
In fact, I can't even stand watching anyone getting tortured.
Kid Chocolate

Kunst und K.o. – wie das Boxen zur Metapher für das Leben wird

Michael Schleicher

Runde 1 – Söhne Kubas

Die Sportler arbeiten. Jeder für sich und doch alle zusammen. Für die nächsten drei Minuten, noch eine Runde Ewigkeit. Sie leben in einer Parallelwelt, mit eigenen Zeiten, nach eigenen Regeln. In Havannas Boxakademie beginnt das Training um vier Uhr in der Früh. »Trommler und Boxer müssen, wollen sie Herausragendes leisten, zeitig beginnen«, hat schließlich im Jahr 1820 der britische Journalist und Autor Pierce Egan (1772–1849) in seiner Textsammlung **Boxania** notiert.[1] Und »zeitig« meint den Start in den Tag ebenso wie das Alter der Athleten.

Die schmucklose Halle scheint zu vibrieren und den Rhythmus der Jungs aufzunehmen. Sie sind hier, um Boxer zu werden. Eines Tages wollen sie die Chancenlosigkeit vor ihre Fäuste nehmen, die das Leben für sie vorgesehen hat. Es ist, als lernten sie mit jeder Bewegung, jedem Schritt, jeder Drehung der Hüfte und jedem Schlag gegen den imaginären Gegner den eigenen Körper besser kennen. Nach und nach erobern sie sich den Raum, modellieren sich selbst in die stickige Luft. Sie schwitzen, pumpen im raschen Wechsel von An- und Entspannung der Muskeln. »Ihr macht das nur für euch, nicht für mich«, schnarrt die Stimme des Trainers. »Drei Minuten noch!« Erneut: eine Ewigkeit.

»Kubanische Boxer kämpfen für eine bessere Zukunft«, sagt Santos Urgelles, einer der jungen Athleten aus der kubanischen Akademie, in Andrew Langs Dokumentarfilm **Sons of Cuba** (2009). Deshalb sind sie hier, deshalb quälen sie sich Runde für Runde. Um über das eigene Schicksal zu triumphieren. Denn von den Gürteln der Weltmeister träumt hier (noch) keiner. Vom glücklichen Leben jedoch alle. Herausboxen wollen sie sich, ihre Herkunft hinter sich lassen, mit schnellen, harten Jabs, mit Uppercuts, die der Kontrahent im besten Fall nicht kommen sieht.

»Wer kann an Medaillen denken, wenn es fast an ein Wunder grenzt, den täglichen Teller Bohnen herbeizuschaffen?«, erinnerte sich Eligio Sardiñas Montalvo (1910–1988) einmal an den Beginn seiner Karriere. Unter seinem Kampfnamen »Kid Chocolate« hat er es 1931 zum Weltmeister im Superfedergewicht gebracht. Eine kubanische Legende, bis heute. Und Vorbild für die Buben zwischen neun und elf Jahren in Havannas Boxschulen: »Wir kämpfen, um jemand zu sein.« Wahrgenommen zu werden – um nichts Geringeres geht es, wenn sich Künstler, Schriftsteller und Filmemacher mit dem Boxsport beschäftigen.

Runde 2 – Boxfilme: Duell mit dem Leben

Seit sich die Menschheit Geschichten erzählt, ist das Duell Mann gegen Mann ein besonderes dramaturgisches Moment. Ob in der Bibel Kain gegen Abel und David gegen Goliath oder der Kampf Menelaos gegen Paris, von dem Homer in seiner **Ilias** berichtet: Der Zweikampf, diese besondere Form der Auseinandersetzung, faszinierte Erzähler und Autoren, ihre Zuhörer und Leser schon immer. Die Germanen kannten den gerichtlichen Zweikampf. Im Mittelalter galt dieser gar

Art and Knockout—When Boxing Becomes a Metaphor for Life

Michael Schleicher

Round 1—Sons of Cuba

The athletes are working. Each for themselves and yet all together. For the next three minutes, another round of eternity. They live in a parallel world with its own times and its own rules. At Havana's boxing academy training starts at 4 a.m. As the British journalist and author, Pierce Egan (1772–1849), noted in 1820 in a collection of his articles titled **Boxania**: "Drummers and boxers, to acquire excellence, must begin young."[1] And they must begin early too.

The austere hall seems to vibrate and pick up the rhythm of the boys. They are here to become boxers. One day they want to get their fists on the lack of opportunities life has provided for them. It is as if with each movement, each step, each hip rotation, and each punch against the imaginary opponent they are getting to know their own bodies better. Little by little they occupy more space, modeling themselves into the stuffy air. They perspire, pumping in the rapid shift between tensing and relaxing their muscles. "You are doing this just for yourselves, not for me," rasps the voice of the trainer. "Three more minutes!" Once again an eternity.

"Cuban boxers fight for a better future," says Santos Urgelles, one of the youngest athletes from the Cuban academy in Andrew Lang's 2009 documentary **Sons of Cuba**. This is why they are here, why they torture themselves round after round— to triumph over their own fate. No one here dreams of the belts of the world champions (yet), but all do of a happy life. They want to box their way out and leave their background behind them, with quick, hard jabs, with uppercuts, ideally of the kind the opponent doesn't see coming.

"Who can think of medals when it is almost a miracle to get one's daily plate of beans?" Eligio Sardiñas Montalvo (1910–88) once reminisced about the beginning of his career. Under his "boxing name," Kid Chocolate, he went on to become junior lightweight champion of the world in 1931. A Cuban legend to this day and a role model for the nine- to eleven-year-old boys in Havana's boxing schools: "We are fighting to be someone." To be noticed—nothing less than this is at stake when artists, writers, and filmmakers reflect on boxing.

Round 2—Boxing Movies: Duel with Life

Ever since mankind has been telling stories, the duel of man versus man has been a dramatically potent moment. Be it Cain vs. Abel and David vs. Goliath in the Bible, or the fight between Menelaus and Paris which Homer relates in his **Iliad**, the duel, this special form of conflict, has always fascinated storytellers and authors as well as their audiences. The Germanic peoples knew the concept of trial by combat, which in the Middle Ages was even considered a divine judgment, and in the 19th century especially honor disputes were settled in duels.

A major change in the tradition of storytelling was brought about by the invention of moving images: from then

als Gottesurteil, und vor allem im 19. Jahrhundert wurden Ehrstreitigkeiten in Duellen aus der Welt geschafft.

Eine wichtige Änderung in der Erzähltradition brachte die Erfindung der bewegten Bilder: Von nun an lag es nicht mehr in der Fantasie des Hörers oder Lesers, wie sich ein Zweikampf abspielte. Regisseure und Schauspieler brachten die Szenen massentauglich auf die Leinwand. So darf etwa bezweifelt werden, dass sich Männer einst tatsächlich im Staub der Straße auf Leben und Tod gegenüberstanden wie Frank (Henry Fonda) und Mundharmonika (Charles Bronson) in Sergio Leones **Spiel mir das Lied vom Tod** aus dem Jahr 1968. Doch hat diese Szene bis heute weder ihre Spannung noch ihre Faszination verloren.

Solche (Italo-)Western sind direkte Vorfahren der Boxfilme, die vor allem in der zweiten Hälfte des 20. Jahrhunderts populär wurden: Produzenten und Regisseure hatten entdeckt, welch narrative Wucht, welche Faszination im Boxen steckt – nicht zuletzt durch die (angebliche) Nähe des Sports zur Halbwelt. Zudem machten Ausnahmeathleten wie Muhammad Ali den Faustkampf bei den Massen beliebt.

Ali erkannte als einer der ersten Boxer den hohen Unterhaltungswert seiner Sportart und gab seinen Kämpfen Titel, die an Blockbuster-Filme erinnern: »Rumble in the Jungle« (1974) oder »Thrilla in Manila (1975). Hollywood hätte sich das nicht besser ausdenken können. Was Ali begann, wirkt bis heute nach. Jeder Fernsehsender, der Boxkämpfe überträgt, wird versuchen, diese mit Bildern, Sequenzen und Sätzen zu bewerben, die an einen Showdown im Kino erinnern.

Zwar ist kaum festzustellen, wie viele Boxfilme bislang gedreht wurden. Aktuell arbeitet Hollywood etwa daran, die Lebensgeschichte von Rocky Marciano (1923–1969) auf die Leinwand zu bringen, dem ersten Weltmeister im Schwergewicht, der seine Karriere ungeschlagen beendet hat und der eines der Vorbilder war für Sylvester Stallones Rocky Balboa. Jeremy Renner (**Mission: Impossible – Rogue Nation**, 2015) soll den italo-amerikanischen Kämpfer spielen; Kinostart von **Undefeated: The Rocky Marciano Story** ist frühestens im Jahr 2017.

Alle Boxfilme verbindet allerdings eines: Sie erzählen Emanzipationsgeschichten. So erlebt der Zuschauer einige Motive immer wieder – egal, ob die Handlung fiktiv ist oder sich an der Vita eines realen Sportlers orientiert. Im Zentrum stehen Figuren, denen etwas fehlt im Leben. Etwas, dass sie innerhalb der Ringseile zu finden hoffen.

Viele Helden boxen sich heraus aus der Unterschicht wie in **Rocky** (1976–2016), **Million Dollar Baby** (2004) oder **The Fighter** (2010). Billy Hope (**Southpaw**, 2015) und Adonis Johnson (**Creed – Rocky's Legacy**, 2015) haben dagegen große Teile ihrer Kindheit elternlos in Heimen verbracht.

Einige Leinwandkämpfer gehören einer ethnischen Minderheit an und müssen sich gegen die Vorurteile der Mehrheit behaupten. Rocky Balboa etwa hat italienische Vorfahren. Micky Ward, Hauptfigur in **The Fighter**, hat irische Wurzeln und die von Michelle Rodríguez gespielte Diana in **Girlfight** (2000) lateinamerikanische. Dieser Film erzählt zudem die Emanzipationsgeschichte einer Frau, die sich in einer Männerdomäne Respekt erkämpft. Ähnlich sieht es für Johanna (Katharina Wackernagel) in der leider vom Publikum kaum wahrgenommenen deutschen Produktion **Die Boxerin** (2006) von Catharina Deus aus. Auch die 19-Jährige muss gegen das Vorurteil antreten, Frauen hätten im Ring nichts verloren. Zudem ist sie Halbwaise und soziale Außenseiterin in der Provinz Brandenburgs kurz nach der Wende 1989/90.

Für all diese Protagonisten gilt, was Sylvester Stallone seinen Rocky im ersten der sieben Filme sagen lässt: »Wenn ich beim Schlussgong immer

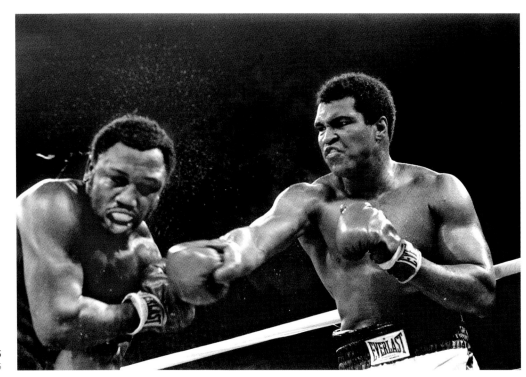

Joe Frazier gegen Muhammad Ali, 1975
Joe Frazier vs. Muhammad Ali, 1975

on the way a duel played out was no longer left to the imagination of the listener or reader. Directors and actors brought the scenes to the screen in ways suitable for mass audiences. It is doubtful, for instance, that men once actually stood face to face in the dust of the street in a duel to the death the way Frank (Henry Fonda) and Harmonica (Charles Bronson) do in Sergio Leone's **Once Upon a Time in the West** (1968). Still, to this day the scene has lost none of its suspense and fascination.

Such (spaghetti) westerns are direct ancestors of the boxing movies that became popular in the second half of the 20th century in particular: producers and directors had discovered the narrative power and fascination that boxing holds, not least because of the sport's (alleged) proximity to racketeering and gangsterism. In addition, exceptional athletes such as Muhammad Ali made boxing popular among the masses.

Ali was one of the first boxers to recognize the great entertainment value of his sport. He gave his fights titles evoking blockbuster movies, such as "Rumble in the Jungle" (1974) and "Thrilla in Manila" (1975). Hollywood couldn't have come up with anything better. What Ali started continues to have an impact today. Every television network broadcasting boxing matches will try to advertise them using images, sequences, and sentences suggesting a showdown in the movies.

It is not easy to determine the number of boxing movies that have been shot to date. Hollywood, for instance, is currently working on bringing the story of Rocky Marciano (1923–69) to the screen, who was the first world heavyweight champion to end his career undefeated and one of the models for Sylvester Stallone's Rocky Balboa. Jeremy Renner (**Mission: Impossible—Rogue Nation**, 2015) will apparently play the Italian American fighter. The earliest release of the movie, **Undefeated: The Rocky Marciano Story**, will be 2017.

All boxing movies do have one thing in common, though: they tell stories of emancipation. As a result, some themes recur over and over again, regardless of whether the plot is fictitious or based on the life of an actual athlete. The focus is on figures that have something lacking in their lives, something they hope to find in the boxing ring.

Many heroes box their way out of the underclass, as in **Rocky** (1976–2016), **Million Dollar Baby** (2004), and **The Fighter** (2010). Billy Hope (**Southpaw**, 2015) and Adonis Johnson (**Creed**, 2015), by contrast, have spent large parts of their childhoods in foster homes.

Some fighters of the silver screen belong to an ethnic minority and are forced to assert themselves against the prejudices of the majority. Rocky Balboa, for instance, has Italian ancestry. Micky Ward, the protagonist of **The Fighter**, has Irish roots, while the origins of Diana (Michelle Rodríguez) in **Girlfight** (2000) are Latin American. The latter film, moreover, tells the story of the emancipation of a woman who earns respect in a male domain. The situation is similar for 19-year-old Johanna (Katharina Wackernagel) in the German production **Die Boxerin** (2006) directed by

Film Still aus *Rocky IV –*
Der Kampf des Jahrhunderts, 1985
Film still from *Rocky IV*, 1985

noch stehe, dann werde ich zum ersten Mal in meinem Leben wissen, dass ich nicht nur irgendein Penner, ein Niemand bin.« Ein Satz, der auch in Kubas Boxschulen fallen könnte. »Wir kämpfen, um jemand zu sein.«

Auf der Leinwand ist der Boxring Katalysator für die Entwicklung einer Figur, hier erfährt sie – oft zum ersten Mal – Bestätigung, lernt Selbstbewusstsein. Im Seilgeviert erkennt der Zuschauer die Lebenslage des Protagonisten in komprimierter Form: Der Gegner wird im Kampf zum Symbol für alles, was im Alltag des Noch-nicht-Helden schiefgelaufen ist oder schiefläuft.

Oft sind das die genannten Herausforderungen. Wobei die Drehbuchautoren diese kombinieren, anreichern: Kämpfe können gegen die eigene, übergriffige Familie ausgefochten werden (**The Fighter**), gegen das eigene Alter (in **Rocky Balboa**, 2006, kehrt der Ex-Weltmeister 60-jährig in den Ring zurück), gegen eine heimtückische, lebensbedrohliche Krankheit (in **Creed – Rocky's Legacy**, erkrankt Rocky, der inzwischen als

Trainer arbeitet, an Krebs) oder gegen den eigenen Jähzorn. Paul Newmans Rocky Graziano landet 1956 in **Die Hölle ist in mir** erst im Knast und scheitert in der Army, bevor er durch das Boxen (Selbst-)Beherrschung lernt. Das gilt auch für Adonis Johnson (Michael B. Jordan) in Ryan Cooglers **Creed – Rocky's Legacy**. Doch der uneheliche Sohn des legendären Schwergewichts-Weltmeisters Apollo Creed muss im siebten Teil der **Rocky**-Reihe nicht nur den Jähzorn in den Griff bekommen, sondern sich auch vom ruhmvollen Ruf seines verstorbenen Vaters befreien. »Ich habe Angst, seinen Namen zu tragen«, sagt er einmal. Gleich zu Beginn des Films ist zu sehen, wie sich Johnson auf einer Leinwand Creeds ersten Kampf gegen Balboa anschaut. Plötzlich steht der junge Mann auf und boxt gegen das Bild seines Erzeugers, ahmt Rockys Schläge nach.

Billy Hope, den das Publikum in **Southpaw** zunächst als Champion kennenlernt, wird zurückgeworfen auf den absoluten Tiefpunkt seines

Seins, um zu wahrer Größe heranreifen zu können: Nach dem Tod seiner Frau stürzt er wirtschaftlich und sozial ab, versumpft in Selbstmitleid und Alkohol, wird gewalttätig, verliert seine Tochter an das Jugendamt und sein Vermögen. Erst das Boxen verleiht Hope wieder Hoffnung.

Misstrauen gegen seine Umwelt prägt auch Jake LaMotta in **Raging Bull – Wie ein wilder Stier** (1980), bevor er sportliche Erfolge feiern darf. Doch Regisseur Martin Scorsese erzählt zudem LaMottas Abstieg, zeigt, wie der Boxer sportlich und menschlich scheitert, weil er sich letztlich doch nicht im Griff hat. Diese Dramaturgie macht die Produktion zu einer Ausnahme unter den Boxfilmen.

Auf der Leinwand wird der Boxring zur Schule des Lebens. Wieder ist es Rocky, der dafür die treffenden Worte findet: »Du und ich – und auch sonst keiner kann so hart zuschlagen wie das Leben. Aber der Punkt ist nicht der, wie hart einer zuschlagen kann. Es zählt bloß, wie viele Schläge man einstecken kann und ob man trotzdem

Catharina Deus, a film that, unfortunately, went largely unnoticed by the public. Johanna has to take on the prejudice that women have no place in the ring. On top of this she has lost a parent and is a social misfit in the backcountry of Brandenburg in East Germany, shortly after the Eastern European upheavals of 1989–90.

True for all of these protagonists is what Sylvester Stallone has his Rocky say in the first of the movies: "If … that bell rings and I'm still standin', I'm gonna know for the first time in my life, see, that I weren't just another bum from the neighborhood." Words that could equally well be uttered in the boxing schools of Cuba. "We are fighting to be someone."

On the movie screen, the boxing ring is the catalyst for a character's development; it is where the character experiences affirmation—often for the first time—and builds self-confidence. In the square circle the situation of the protagonist reveals itself in compressed form to the viewer: during the fight the opponent becomes a symbol of everything that has gone wrong—or is going wrong—in the everyday life of the hero-to-be.

These are oftentimes the aforementioned challenges, with the screenwriters combining and adding to them: battles may be fought against the

protagonist's own abusive family (**The Fighter**), against the protagonist's own age (in the 2006 movie **Rocky Balboa**, the former world champion returns to the ring as a 60-year-old), against an insidious, life-threatening disease (in **Creed**, Rocky, who is now working as a trainer, learns he has non-Hodgkin's lymphoma) or against the protagonist's own violent temper.

Paul Newman's Rocky Graziano, in the 1956 movie **Somebody Up There Likes Me**, first ends up in prison and screws up in the army, before he learns to control his temper through boxing. The same is true for Adonis Johnson (Michael B. Jordan) in Ryan Coogler's **Creed**. However, the illegitimate son of legendary world heavyweight champion Apollo Creed in the seventh installment of the **Rocky** series must not only learn to control his temper, but also cast off the illustrious reputation of his deceased father. "I am afraid of taking on the name," he says at one point. At the very beginning of the film we see Johnson watching Creed's first fight against Balboa on the creen. Suddenly, the young man gets up and starts boxing against the image of his progenitor, imitating Rocky's punches.

Billy Hope, whom the audience initially gets to know as a champion in **Southpaw**, is thrown back into the absolute nadir of his existence, before

being able to mature to true greatness: following the death of his wife he runs aground financially and socially, becomes mired in self-pity and alcohol, resorts to violence, loses his daughter to child protection services, and loses his money. Only boxing gives Billy his hope back again.

Mistrust of his environment also shapes Jake LaMotta in **Raging Bull** (1980), before he is able to celebrate successes in the boxing ring. But director Martin Scorsese also tells of LaMotta's decline, and shows how the boxer fails both as an athlete and as a human being due to his ultimate lack of self-control. It is a storyline that makes the movie exceptional among boxing films.

On screen, the boxing ring becomes a school of life. Once again it is Rocky who puts it best: "You, me, or nobody is gonna hit as hard as life. But it ain't about how hard ya hit. It's about how hard you can get hit and keep moving forward. How much you can take and keep moving forward. That's how winning is done!" So as they box, the protagonists learn that any problem can be solved by working hard on oneself both mentally and physically. Incidentally, the pathos imbuing Balboa's words is commonly found wherever art, commerce, and boxing meet.

weitermacht. Nur so gewinnt man.« Beim Boxen lernen die Protagonisten also, dass sich jedes Problem durch harte psychische und physische Arbeit mit und an sich selbst lösen lässt. Das Pathos, das Balboas Sätze tränkt, ist übrigens häufig zu finden, wenn Kunst, Kommerz und Faustkampf aufeinandertreffen.

Einige Regisseure versuchen, Politik und Boxen zu verweben. Das funktioniert vor allem, wenn die Realität das Drehbuch schreibt: Michael Manns Biopic **Ali** aus dem Jahr 2001 erzählt eben nicht nur das Leben von Cassius Clay, sondern auch Muhammad Alis Emanzipation als Afroamerikaner, als zum Islam konvertierter Christ, als Army-Verweigerer während des Vietnamkriegs mit den wohl wichtigsten Sätzen seines Lebens: »Man, I ain't got no quarrel with them Vietcong. No Vietcong ever called me nigger.«

Peinlich kann es indes werden, wenn fiktive Geschichten um politische Parolen gestrickt werden. **Rocky IV – Der Kampf des Jahrhunderts** von 1985 ist bis dato der mieseste Tiefschlag: Der faire US-Amerikaner tritt gegen den mit allen unerlaubten Mitteln kämpfenden Sowjetrussen Ivan Drago an, nachdem dieser Rockys Freund bei einem Schaukampf (!) getötet (!!) hat. Eine Produktion voller westlicher Vorurteile, Klischees und Propaganda in Zeiten des Kalten Kriegs, die 1986 mit gleich fünf Goldenen Himbeeren abgestraft wurde, dem Anti-Preis für die schlechtesten Leistungen im Filmgeschäft.

Die bis heute radikalste Emanzipationsgeschichte hat dagegen Clint Eastwood in seinem mit vier Oscars ausgezeichneten **Million Dollar Baby** erzählt. Er beginnt mit der klassischen Dramaturgie des Genres, zeigt eine aus ärmlichen Verhältnissen stammende Frau, die eigentlich zu alt fürs Boxen ist und sich dennoch an die Spitze kämpft. Dann aber fokussiert Eastwood etwas vollkommen anderes: Nach einem Unfall ist seine Heldin Maggie unheilbar gelähmt ans Krankenbett gefesselt. Sie kämpft jedoch weiter – jetzt um ihr Recht auf einen selbstbestimmten Tod. Sie kämpft diesen Kampf gegen ihren Trainer, gegen ihre Freunde, gegen ihre Familie und gegen das Gesetz, das Sterbehilfe unter Strafe verbietet. Am Ende des Films verlässt Maggie dennoch siegreich den Ring des Lebens.

Runde 3 – Stairway to Heaven

Was im Kriegsfilm der Hügel, den jede siegreiche Truppe im Lauf der Handlung überwinden muss, ist im Boxfilm die Treppe. Um seinen Platz im Ring (und damit im Leben) zu finden und zu behaupten, muss der Held so manche Stufe erklimmen. Die vielleicht berühmteste Treppe der Kinogeschichte ist jene, die hoch zum Philadelphia Museum of Art führt. Hier trainiert Rocky Balboa im ersten Teil der Reihe 1976 – und spätestens seit damals ist das Treppenmotiv dramaturgisches Element eines jeden Boxfilms.

Besonders virtuos spielt Regisseur Antoine Fuqua in **Southpaw** (2015) mit diesem Topos. Etwa nach der Hälfte des Films hat Billy Hope (Jake Gyllenhaal), der ehemalige Champion im Halbschwergewicht, alles verloren: seine Frau, seine Tochter, sein Vermögen, sein Heim, seinen Gürtel, seine Selbstachtung. Der Mann ist am Boden und scheint immer tiefer zu fallen. Der Weg zurück ins Leben führt – wie kann es anders sein – über den Boxring. Als Hope endlich wieder mit dem Training beginnen will, besucht er das Gym des Trainers Tick Wills (Forest Whitaker). Nicht zufällig erinnert dessen Nachname an die Zeile

Some directors try to weave together politics and boxing. This tends to work especially when reality writes the script. Thus Michael Mann's 2001 biopic **Ali** recounts not just the life of Cassius Clay, but also Muhammad Ali's emancipation as an African American, as a Christian who converted to Islam, and as a draft dodger at the time of the Vietnam War, uttering what may have been the most important words of his life: "Man, I ain't got no quarrel with them Vietcong. No Vietcong ever called me nigger."

When fictitious stories are woven around political slogans, it can become embarrassing, though. **Rocky IV** (1985) is the ugliest low blow to date in this regard: in the "Fight of the Century" the decent US boxer takes on Ivan Drago from the Soviet Union who fights by any unfair means and has, in fact, previously killed Rocky's friend—in an exhibition fight, no less. It is a movie rife with Western prejudices, stereotypes, and propaganda at the time of the Cold War, which in 1986 was punished with as many as five Golden Raspberries for the worst performances in film.

The most radical story of emancipation to date, however, is the one told by Clint Eastwood in **Million Dollar Baby**, winner of four Oscars. He starts out with the classic storyline of the genre, showing a woman from a poor background who is really too old to box and yet fights her way to the top. But then Eastwood focuses on something altogether different: after an accident, his heroine, Maggie, is permanently paralyzed and bed-ridden. She continues to fight, though—this time for her right to choose her own death. She fights this battle against her trainer, her friends, her own family, and against the law that makes assisted suicide a punishable offense. At the end of the movie Maggie nevertheless leaves the ring of life triumphantly.

Round 3—Stairway to Heaven

The hill to be overcome at some point of the story by victorious troops is to war movies what stairs are to the boxing movie. To find and keep his place in the ring (and, consequently, in life), the hero has to climb many a step. Arguably the most famous steps in the history of cinema are the ones leading up to the Philadelphia Museum of Art. This is where Rocky Balboa works out in the first installment of the series from 1976, and ever since then stairs have been a dramatic feature of every boxing movie.

Director Antoine Fuqua plays brilliantly with this motif in **Southpaw**. About halfway into the movie, Billy Hope (Jake Gyllenhaal), the former light-heavyweight champion, has lost everything: his wife, his daughter, his money, his home, his belt, his self-respect. The man is bummed out and seems to fall deeper and deeper. The way back to life leads—who would have guessed it?—through the boxing ring. When Hope finally wants to start training again, he visits the gym of trainer Tick Wills (Forest Whitaker). It is no coincidence that the latter's surname evokes the words "Just a man and his will to survive" from the song **Eye of the Tiger**, which was written by the rock band Survivor for **Rocky III**, made in 1982.

In a single, cleverly composed scene Fuqua and his cinematographer show the arduous but ultimately positive progress the boxer will make—and with him the film. The gym is located on the second floor and the staircase leading up to it is narrow and steep. When Hope enters from the street, the camera looks down at him from the top of the stairs; he is barely visible in the twilight, especially since the door just closes behind him. This shot shows viewers a nobody who is literally no longer visible, and who has a long and uncomfortable road ahead of him.

This impression is reinforced when Hope starts climbing the stairs in the next scene. Fiore's camera is now right behind him and follows him on his way up: there the boxer steps from the

»Just a man and his will to survive« aus dem Song **Eye of the Tiger**, den die Band Survivor 1982 für **Rocky III** komponiert hat.

Die anstrengende, doch letztlich positive Entwicklung, die der Boxer und damit der Film nehmen wird, zeigen Fuqua und sein Kameramann Mauro Fiore in einer einzigen, klug komponierten Szene: Das Gym liegt im ersten Stock, schmal und steil ist das Treppenhaus, das nach oben führt. Als Hope von der Straße hereinkommt, blickt die Kamera von der oberen Stufe zu ihm hinunter; kaum zu erahnen ist er im Dämmerlicht, zumal gerade die Tür hinter ihm zufällt. Diese Einstellung präsentiert dem Zuschauer einen Niemand, der im wahrsten Wortsinn nicht mehr gesehen wird und vor dem ein langer, ungemütlicher Weg liegt.

Dieser Eindruck wird verstärkt, als Hope sich in der nächsten Sequenz daranmacht, die Stufen zum Trainingsraum hinaufzusteigen. Fiores Kamera ist nun direkt hinter ihm und folgt ihm nach oben: Aus dem Dunkel heraus ins Helle läuft der Boxer da, denn gegenüber der Tür, hinter der trainiert wird, befindet sich das einzige Fenster in diesem Treppenhaus. Die grelle Sonne beleuchtet den Eingang zum Gym und kündet vom allbekannten Licht am Ende des Tunnels. Nur das Boxen, erzählt diese

Bildgestaltung, ist noch in der Lage, Hopes Leben zum Guten zu wenden.

Später nutzt der Regisseur das Treppenmotiv in einer ungewöhnlichen Variation: Hope muss zunächst Hausmeisteraufgaben übernehmen, um Tick Wills zu überzeugen, dass er sein Comeback ernst meint. Gerade als er eine Leiter hinaufgestiegen ist, um eine defekte Neonröhre auszutauschen, tritt Wills zu ihm: »Wir fangen morgen an.« - »Was denn? Training??«, fragt Hope ungläubig. »Nein. Ponyreiten«, kontert der Trainer trocken. Hope weiß, dass er die erste Prüfung bestanden hat – just in diesem Moment springt die Deckenleuchte an. »Alles hell und klar«, stellt der Boxer fest – und meint auch sein eigenes Schicksal.

In **Creed – Rocky's Legacy** erfolgt die Initiation des Boxers ebenfalls über Treppenstufen: Hier geht Adonis Johnson zunächst aus dem Keller einer Kneipe in Tijuana zu einem mehr oder minder legalen Kampf hinauf, und so energisch, wie er sich bewegt, so dicht, wie ihm die Kamera folgt, ist klar, dass hier einer sein Potenzial verschenkt: Dieser Kämpfer hat mehr drauf, als zum Gaudium der Besoffenen andere zu verprügeln. Doch ist es ein weiter Weg von Mexiko bis zum Titelkampf. Und erst nach dem Schlussgong lässt Regisseur

Coogler seinen Protagonisten – zusammen mit dessen Trainer – vor jenen 72 Steinstufen stehen, die längst verankert sind im popkulturellen Gedächtnis der Welt. Die beiden steigen hoch, sichtlich angestrengt. Und als sie endlich oben vor dem Philadelphia Museum of Art stehen, da fehlt ihnen die Kraft zur Siegerpose. Oder?

Runde 4 – der doppelte Jack

Keine Frage: Bevor es im Kino überhaupt denkbar war, dass Rocky mit seinem afroamerikanischen Schützling Johnson nach dessen WM-Kampf gegen Ricky Conlan (den der britische Cruisergewichtler Tony Bellew spielt) die Freitreppe vor dem Kunsttempel in Philadelphia erklimmt, brauchte es einen ganz anderen Johnson. Jack Johnson. Ohne dessen Leistung dürften sich auch Kubas junge Talente heute kaum Hoffnungen auf einen Weltmeistergürtel machen.

John Arthur »Jack« Johnson (1878–1946) war der erste schwarze Champion im Schwergewicht. Sein Sieg zu Beginn des 20. Jahrhunderts wurde als Ungeheuerlichkeit verstanden, die den Rassismus nicht nur in den USA einmal mehr offen zu Tage treten ließ. Es hatte gedauert, bis Johnson, in Texas als Sohn ehemaliger Sklaven geboren, seine Chance erhielt. Alles hatte Weltmeister Tommy

dark into the light, as the only window in this stairwell is across from the door to the gym. The glaring sun lights the entrance to the gym and heralds the proverbial light at the end of the tunnel. Only boxing, this image suggests, can still turn Hope's life around.

Later on, the director employs the motif of stairs in an unusual variation: Hope first has to take on janitorial work to convince Tick Wills that he is serious about his comeback. Just as he climbs on a ladder to replace a broken neon tube, Wills walks over to him and says: "We start tomorrow." "What? Our training?" Hope asks incredulously. "No. Baking cookies," the trainer retorts dryly. Hope knows he has passed the first test and at this very moment the overhead light clicks on. "Shining so bright," the boxer notes, referring also to his own fate. In **Creed** the boxer's initiation occurs via stairs as well. Adonis Johnson walks up from the basement of a bar in Tijuana to a more or less legal fight, and considering how energetically he moves and how closely the camera follows him, it is obvious that this is someone who is wasting his potential: this fighter could do a lot more than

beat up others to amuse the drunks. But it is a long road from Mexico to the title bout. And only after the final bell does the director put his protagonist—along with his trainer—in front of those 72 steps, which have long etched themselves into global pop-cultural memory. The two climb up the steps, visibly laboring. And when they finally stand at the top in front of the Philadelphia Museum of Art, they lack the strength to strike a victory pose. Or do they?

Round 4—The Double Jack

No doubt about it: before it became conceivable in the movies for Rocky to climb the steps in front of Philadelphia's temple to art with Johnson, his African-American protégé, after the latter's title bout against Ricky Conlan (played by British cruiserweight Tony Bellew), a very different Johnson was needed. Jack Johnson, that is. Without his achievements there would be little hope of ever winning a world champion belt even for today's young Cuban talents.

John Arthur "Jack" Johnson (1878–1946) was the first black heavyweight champion. His triumph at the beginning of the 20th century was seen as

an outrage which once again exposed racism, not just in the US. It took a while before Johnson, who was born in Texas, the son of former slaves, got his chance. World champion Tommy Burns (1881–1955) had tried everything to avoid a bout with the southpaw who was over 6 feet tall.

On Saturday, December 26, 1908, the two athletes finally faced each other in the ring in Sydney, Australia. As the German writer and boxing fan, Wolf Wondratschek, wrote retrospectively: "Black America is at this point boxing toward its future—after all, the blacks, in particular, will be the ones to excel in this sport. But no reasonable person at the time was willing to console themselves with such prophecies."[2] More than 20,000 spectators watched the bout, which was stopped by the police in the fourteenth round and made Johnson world champion. The seemingly superior white race had lost. "This was yet another one of those times, where history and boxing, specifically the heavyweight championship, intersected in the most interesting and electrifying way," David Remnick, editor-in-chief of the **New Yorker**, author, and Ali biographer wrote more than a century later to

Burns (1881–1955) versucht, um dem Kampf mit dem 1,87 Meter großen Linksausleger auszuweichen.

Am 26. Dezember 1908, einem Samstag, standen sich die beiden Athleten dann endlich im australischen Sydney im Ring gegenüber. »Das schwarze Amerika boxt sich zwar in diesem Moment seiner Zukunft entgegen – denn es werden ja vor allem die Schwarzen sein, die sich in diesem Sport hervortun –, aber kein vernünftiger Mensch wollte sich damals schon mit solchen Prophezeiungen trösten«,[2] schreibt der boxbegeisterte Dichter Wolf Wondratschek rückblickend. Mehr als 20 000 Zuschauer sahen den Kampf, der in der 14. Runde von der Polizei abgebrochen wurde und Johnson zum Weltmeister machte. Die scheinbar so überlegene weiße Rasse hatte verloren. »This was yet another one of those times, where history and boxing, specifically the heavyweight championship, intersected in the most interesting and electrifying way«, erklärt David Remnick, Chefredakteur des »New Yorker«, Autor und Ali-Biograf, gut 100 Jahre später die gesellschaftspolitische Bedeutung dieses Sportereignisses.

Im Publikum um den Ring im Stadion von Sydney saß damals auch der US-amerikanische Schriftsteller Jack London (1876–1916). Der Autor

von Werken wie **Ruf der Wildnis** (1903) und **Seewolf** (1904) hatte im Jahr 1905 mit **The Game** seine erste von vier Kurzgeschichten vorgelegt, die vom Boxen erzählen. Es folgten **A Piece of Steak** (1909), **The Mexican** (1911) sowie **The Abysmal Brute** (1911). Den Titelkampf Burns vs. Johnson beobachtete London als Reporter des »New York Herald«; seine Reportage wurde – teilweise variiert – auch in anderen Blättern gedruckt, etwa dem in San Francisco erscheinenden »The Call«.

Der boxbegeisterte Schriftsteller zeigt sich in diesen Texten als Kind seiner Zeit: »Personally, I was with Burns all the way. He is a white man, and so am I. Naturally I wanted to see the white man win«, heißt es in seinem Beitrag, den die damals in Melbourne erscheinende Tageszeitung »The Argus« am 28. Dezember 1908 veröffentlichte. Doch London war eben auch Faustkampfexperte; als solcher hält er wenige Zeilen später fest: »Because a white man wishes the white man to win should not prevent him from giving absolute credit to the best man, who did win, even when that best man was black. All hail to Johnson!«

Egal, in welchem Text man weiterliest: Der damals bereits angesehene Autor (die »Argus«-Redaktion überschrieb den Beitrag in Versalien mit »FAMOUS NOVELIST'S ACCOUNT«)

schildert den Kampf sachverständig, bildreich und durchaus bewundernd für den farbigen Herausforderer: »Johnson play-acted all the time. His part was the clown, and he played with Burns from the gong of the opening round to the finish of the fight. Burns was a toy in his hands. For Johnson it was a kindergarten romp.«

Der Boxring ein Kindergarten-Spielplatz? Die Überlegenheit des Herausforderers muss erdrückend gewesen sein. Seinen Artikel für den »Call« beginnt London mit folgenden Sätzen – und selbst heute noch meint man, seine Fassungslosigkeit zu hören: »The fight; there was no fight. No Armenian massacre could compare with the hopeless slaughter that took place in the Sydney stadium today. It was not a case of ›Too Much Johnson‹, but of all Johnson. A golden smile tells the story; and a golden smile was Johnson's.«

Dieses »goldene Lächeln« des schwarzen Boxers muss die weißen Zuschauer besonders provoziert haben: Johnson hatte sich seine Zähne durch goldene ersetzen lassen. Er grinste ins Publikum und ärgerte seinen hoffnungslos überforderten Gegner. Einmal, schreibt London, habe der Herausforderer den Weltmeister angehalten, ihm in den ungeschützten

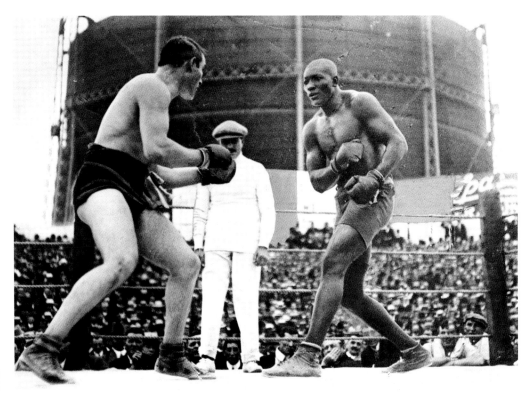

Tommy Burns gegen Jack Johnson, 1908
Tommy Burns vs. Jack Johnson, 1908

explain to socio-political significance of this sporting event.

Among the ringside spectators in the Sydney stadium at the time was American writer Jack London (1876–1916). In 1905, the author of works such as **The Call of the Wild** (1903) and **The Sea Wolf** (1904) had produced the first of four short stories about boxing titled "The Game." This was followed by "A Piece of Steak" (1909), "The Mexican" (1911), and "The Abysmal Brute" (1911). London attended the title fight Burns vs. Johnson as a reporter of the **New York Herald**; his report was published—with modifications—in other papers as well, including in the San Francisco-based **The Call**.

In those texts the writer and boxing enthusiast appears as a child of his times: "Personally, I was with Burns all the way. He is a white man, and so am I. Naturally I wanted to see the white man win," he wrote in an article that was published two days after the fight by the Melbourne-based daily **The Argus**. But London was a boxing expert as well and as such he noted a few lines further down: "Be-cause a white man wishes the white man to win should not prevent him from giving absolute credit to the best man, who did win, even when that best man was black. All hail to Johnson!"

No matter which text one continues reading, the author, who was already renowned at the time (the editors of **The Argus** added an all-caps headline to his article, which read FAMOUS NOVELIST'S ACCOUNT), expertly and graphically described the fight—and not without admiration for the black challenger: "Johnson play-acted all the time. His part was the clown, and he played with Burns from the gong of the opening round to the finish of the fight. Burns was a toy in his hands. For Johnson it was a kindergarten romp."

The boxing ring a kindergarten playground? The challenger's superiority must have been crushing. London begins his article for **The Call** with the following remarks—and even today it feels like we hear his consternation: "The fight; there was no fight. No Armenian massacre could compare with the hopeless slaughter that took place in the Sydney stadium today. It was not a case of 'Too Much Johnson,' but of all Johnson. A golden smile tells the story; and a golden smile was Johnson's."

The black boxer's "golden smile" must have been particularly provoking to the white spectators: Johnson had had his teeth replaced with golden ones. He grinned at the audience and provoked his hopelessly overwhelmed opponent. At one point, London writes, the challenger encouraged the world champion to punch him in his unprotected stomach. Burns walked right into the trap and struck a blow—"John-son would neither wince nor cover up"—an at the time outrageous show of force by the allegedly gutless, feeble black race.

Jack London ultimately found fault with the victorious Johnson only for not having knocked out Burns in the thirteenth round, even though it would have been "child's play." Yet at the same time he called for revenge for this humiliation of his own skin color and recovery of the title by a white man. His appeal was directed at James J. Jeffries (1875–1953) who had retired

Jess Willard gegen Jack Johnson, 1915
Jess Willard vs. Jack Johnson, 1915

Bauch zu schlagen. Burns tappte in die Falle, schlug zu – »Johnson would neither wince nor cover up«. Eine für damalige Zeiten ungeheuerliche Machtdemonstration der angeblich feigen, schwächlichen schwarzen Rasse.

Während Jack London am Ende dem siegreichen Johnson sportlich nur einen Fehler ankreidete – in der 13. Runde Burns nicht k. o. geschlagen zu haben, obwohl es ein »child's play« gewesen wäre –, forderte er zugleich Vergeltung für die Demütigung der eigenen Hautfarbe und die Rückholung des Titels durch einen Weißen. Sein Appell richtete sich an James J. Jeffries (1875–1953), der 1905 als Schwergewichts-Champion zurückgetreten war und sich auf seine Farm zurückgezogen hatte. »But one thing remains. Jeffries must emerge from his alfalfa farm and remove that smile from Johnson's face. Jeff, it's up to you.« Doch auch dem als »Great White Hope« titulierten Jeffries sollte es 1910 nicht gelingen, das Lächeln aus Johnsons Gesicht zu tilgen.

Erst am 5. April 1915 verlor Jack Johnson seinen Titel – unter der heißen Sonne Kubas. Nach Augenzeugenberichten verfolgten rund 25 000 Menschen den auf 45 Runden angelegten Kampf gegen Jess Willard (1881–1968) im Oriental Park Racetrack in Havanna. Johnson ging in der 26. Runde k. o. – und seit damals wird darüber gestritten, ob der Kampf gekauft war: Floss Bestechungsgeld, wurde ihm mit einem Attentat gedroht oder war es das versprochene Visum für die Einreise in die USA, um die kranke Mutter nochmals zu sehen? Als Beweis dafür, dass an jenem Nachmittag auf Kuba nicht alles mit rechten Dingen zugegangen sein konnte, gilt vielen ein Foto, das den Moment nach dem Knockout dokumentiert: Johnson liegt auf dem Rücken, an seinem Kopfende steht der Ringrichter, zählt ihn an. Klar zu erkennen ist, dass der Boxer Arme und Fäuste vor dem Gesicht gekreuzt hält – schützt Johnson in diesem Moment seine Augen vor dem gleißenden Sonnenlicht? Eine überflüssige, ja ihm eigentlich unmögliche Geste, hätte Willard seinen Kontrahenten tatsächlich in die tiefe Dunkelheit eines Knockouts geschickt. Wie auch immer: Der Gürtel war zurück in den Fäusten eines weißen Schwergewichtlers, bis Joe Louis 1937 in der achten Runde Jim Braddock in den Ringstaub schickte.

Johnson stieg dann 1916 in Barcelona nochmals in die Faustkampfarena – gegen den vogelwilden britischen Poeten und am Rande des Wahnsinns tänzelnden Amateurboxer Arthur Cravan, den »König der verkrachten Existenzen«. Es ging beiden wohl vor allem ums Geld – und Cravan relativ rasch auf die Bretter. Was den Schriftsteller Wolf Wondratschek Jahrzehnte später zur lakonischen Feststellung veranlasste: »Der Surrealist hatte die Realität eines Kinnhakens kennengelernt.«[3]

Miles Davis (1926–1991), Boxfan, befreundet mit Sugar Ray Robinson (1921–1989) und Hobby-Faustkämpfer (»Don't hit me in the mouth. I gotta play tonight.«), würdigte im Jahr 1970 Jack Johnsons sportliche Leistung und dessen Verdienste um die Gleichberechtigung dunkelhäutiger Menschen. Damals nahm der Jazztrompeter

as heavyweight champion in 1905 and retreated to his farm. "But one thing remains. Jeffries must emerge from his alfalfa farm and remove that smile from Johnson's face. Jeff, it's up to you." In 1910 Jeffries, a.k.a the "Great White Hope," would have a chance to do so, but he, too, failed.

Jack Johnson only lost his title on April 5, 1915—under the hot Cuban sun. According to eyewitness reports, some 25,000 people watched the 45-round bout against Jess Willard (1881–1968) at the Oriental Park Racetrack in Havana. Johnson was knocked out in the twenty-sixth round, and ever since it has been debated whether the fight was fixed: did bribe money change hands, was there a threat against his life, or was it the visa he was promised to go back to the US and see his sick mother once more? A photograph documenting the moment after the knockout is considered by many to be proof that things in Cuba had been not quite kosher: Johnson is lying on his back and the referee is standing by his head and has started counting. One can clearly see that the boxer holds his arms and fists crossed in front of his face: is Johnson protecting his eyes against the glittering sunlight at this moment? This gesture would have been superfluous and,

indeed, impossible for him to make, if Willard had actually sent him into the deep darkness of a knockout. Anyway, the belt was back in the hands of a white heavyweight, until Joe Louis laid Jim Braddock on the canvas in the eighth round in 1937.

Johnson entered the boxing arena once more in Barcelona in 1916, against the wild British poet and borderline-crazy amateur boxer Arthur Cravan, the "king of failures." For both the fight was probably above all about the money—and for Cravan about hitting the canvas rather quickly, which decades later prompted the German writer Wolf Wondratschek to observe laconically: "The surrealist had become acquainted with the reality of an uppercut."[3]

In 1970, Miles Davis (1926–91), who was a boxing fan and friends with Sugar Ray Robinson (1921–89) as well as a hobby boxer himself ("Don't hit me in the mouth. I gotta play tonight"), paid tribute to Jack Johnson's athletic performance and his contribution to the struggle for black equality. At that time the jazz trumpeter ("Boxing's got style like music's got style") recorded the album **A Tribute to Jack Johnson** with a line-up of top-class musicians (including John McLaughlin on the guitar and Herbie Hancock at the keyboards), which was released

by Columbia in 1971. The music served as the soundtrack for a 1970 documentary about Johnson directed by Jim Jacobs. A few years ago, Tim Cumming encapsulated the historical circumstances that informed the album's making and its significance in **The Guardian**: "It is a record galvanised by boxing, funk, politics, black power, hard rock and the white heat of a creative peak in the recording studio that extended from early 1969 to the summer of 1970." At the end of the piece "Yesternow," Davis had the actor Brock Peters speak Johnson's words: "I'm Jack Johnson—heavyweight champion of the world! I'm black! They never let me forget it. I'm black all right; I'll never let them forget it."

Round 5—Adoration and Mockery in Antiquity

Jack Johnson, his "golden smile," his talent, and the abuse he had to endure are history. They have become part of the great narrative tradition of this sport, bygone but still present to aficionados. When American journalist and essayist A.J. Liebling (1904–63) talked about boxing, a sport he loved, and on which he wrote more knowledgeably than most, he liked to use the phrase "sweet science." Borrowing from the aforementioned journalist Pierce Egan ("the sweet science of

Miles Davis,
A Tribute to Jack Johnson, LP cover

(»Boxing's got style like music's got style.«) mit einer hochkarätigen Besetzung (unter anderen John McLaughlin an der Gitarre und Herbie Hancock, der an den Keyboards saß) das Album **A Tribute to Jack Johnson** auf, das 1971 bei Columbia erschien. Regisseur Jim Jacobs nutzte die Musik für seinen Dokumentarfilm über Johnson. »It is a record galvanised by boxing, funk, politics, black power, hard rock and the white heat of a creative peak in the recording studio that extended from early 1969 to the summer of 1970«, fasste Tim Cumming vor einigen Jahren im »Guardian« die Zeitumstände der Entstehung und die Bedeutung des Albums zusammen. Am Ende des Stücks »Yesternow« ließ Davis den Schauspieler Brock Peters diese Sätze Johnsons sprechen: »I'm Jack Johnson – heavyweight champion of the world! I'm black! They never let me forget it. I'm black all right; I'll never let them forget it.«

Runde 5 – Verehrung und Spott in der Antike

Jack Johnson, sein »goldenes Lächeln«, sein Talent und die Schmähungen, die er erdulden musste, sind Geschichte. Eingegangen in die große Erzähltradition dieses Sports – vergangen, doch bei Aficionados noch immer gegenwärtig. Wenn A. J. Liebling (1904–1963)

vom Boxen sprach, das er liebte und über das er so kenntnisreich schrieb wie wenig andere seiner Zeit, dann nutzte der US-amerikanische Journalist und Essayist mit Vorliebe die Formulierung »Sweet Science«. Diesen Titel, den er sich beim bereits genannten Journalisten Pierce Egan ausgeborgt hatte (»the sweet science of bruising«), gab Liebling seiner Textsammlung über den Faustkampf, die 1956 erstmals als Buch erschien und heute ein Klassiker der Boxliteratur ist. Im Zentrum dieser Feuilletons stehen die Fünfzigerjahre, als die Herrschaft von Joe Louis im Schwergewicht endete und Rocky Marciano den Thron bestieg. Doch Liebling, der selbst gerne im Ring stand, bettete seine Texte stets in die Historie des Sports ein. Allein das macht seine Beiträge nach wie vor lesenswert. »Die artige

Kunst«, schreibt er an einer Stelle, »ist mit der Vergangenheit auf so natürliche Weise verbunden wie der Arm eines Mannes mit seiner Schulter.«[4]

Eines der eindrucksvollsten Zeugnisse dieser Vergangenheit wurde im Jahr 1885 während Bauarbeiten am Quirinalshügel in Rom entdeckt: die griechische Bronzestatue eines Boxers. Ihre Entstehung datiert die Wissenschaft auf die zweite Hälfte des 4. Jahrhunderts v. Chr. oder auf das dritte vorchristliche Jahrhundert; aufgrund ihres Fundorts wird die Arbeit gemeinhin auch der »Faustkämpfer vom Quirinal« genannt. Wie der Archäologe Vinzenz Brinkmann darlegt, »herrscht in der Forschung kein Konsens zur Deutung der Figur. Sie wird als Athletenbild, aber auch als Darstellung eines mythischen Heroen angesprochen.«[5]

bruising"), Liebling used it as the title for his collection of texts about pugilism that was first published as a book in 1956, and is nowadays considered a classic of boxing literature. The feature articles focus on the 1950s when Joe Louis's reign as heavyweight champion ended and Rocky Marciano ascended the throne. Yet Liebling, who liked to be in the ring himself, always embedded his texts in the history of the sport. This alone still makes his articles worth reading today. "The Sweet Science," he writes at one point, "is joined onto the past like a man's arm to his shoulder."[4]

Particularly impressive evidence of this past was discovered when a Greek bronze statue of a boxer was unearthed during construction work on the Quirinal Hill in Rome in 1885. Scholars date the sculpture to the second half of the fourth or the third century BCE; called **Boxer at Rest**, it is also commonly referred to as the "Boxer of the Quirinal," because of the site where it was found. As the archaeologist Vinzenz Brinkmann explains: "There is no consensus among scholars as to how to interpret the figure. Some view it as the image of an athlete, others as the representation of a mythical hero."[5]

The depiction of the boxer is fascinating, for pugilism was considered one of the toughest sports in antiquity. "Probably this is precisely why boxing was a sport favored by the aristocracy. As early as 688 BCE, boxers appear on the lists of winners of ancient Olympia and early on honorific statues of the victors were erected at sanctuaries and in the market squares of their native towns."[6]

Held at the Museo Nazionale Romano, the roughly 51-inch-tall **Boxer at Rest** depicts a sitting athlete, probably just after a fight. In ancient pugilism there were no rounds; instead, boxers fought literally till they dropped. It is easy to see that our boxer is breathing through his mouth, which suggests a major effort immediately preceding the moment and/or blood in his nose. He is looking up over his right shoulder and his arms are resting on his thighs. His hands are protected by gloves that have chiseled leather straps tied into them—to increase the impact of his own punches and, consequently, the risk of injury for the opponent.

Unlike the athlete's well-trained and intact—though bloodied—body (in ancient boxing only punches to the head were allowed, which often led to eyes and teeth being brutally damaged), his face shows evidence of past and current fights: his nose is flat, as if it had been broken at least once; the eyes, which are set deep in their sockets, are swollen; wounds are bleeding. To enhance this effect the sculptor used "colored inlays that indicate the serious wounds to the face and the ears, as well as the blood dripping from the head down the shoulders, the right upper arm and the right thigh, in copper. A bruise underneath the right eye was cast separately in a special alloy and inlaid."[7] For Edilberto Formigli the statue is, indeed, the "only proven example to date of coloring through the use of different alloys."[8]

What the ancient artist tried to achieve with variously colored metals was translated into verse in a satirical poem about a boxer named Stratophon by the 1st-century Greek grammarian and poet Lucilius, who liked to write about boxers in particular:

"When Ulysses after twenty years came safe to his home / Argos, the dog, recognized his appearance when he saw him, / but you, Stratophon, after boxing for four hours, / have become not only unrecognizable to dogs but to the city. / If you trouble to look at your face in the glass, / you will say on your oath: 'I am not Stratophon.'"[9]

These are not the only lines in which the poet describes the brutal disfigurements that characterized pugilists

Spannend ist die Darstellung des Boxers, denn der Faustkampf galt in der Antike als eine der härtesten Sportarten. »Vermutlich war das Boxen gerade auch deshalb ein vom Adel bevorzugter Sport. Schon seit 688 v. Chr. erscheinen die Boxer auf den Siegerlisten von Olympia, und früh schon wurden den Siegern in den Heiligtümern und auf den heimischen Marktplätzen Ehrenstatuen errichtet.«[6]

Der »Faustkämpfer vom Quirinal« – die rund 1,30 Meter hohe Statue befindet sich heute im Museo Nazionale Romano – zeigt einen sitzenden Athleten, vermutlich kurz nach einem Kampf; das antike Boxen kannte keine Runden. Es wurde sprichwörtlich bis zum Umfallen geboxt. Unschwer zu erkennen ist, dass er durch den Mund atmet, was auf eine dem Moment unmittelbar vorausgegangene große Anstrengung schließen lässt – und/oder auf Blut in der Nase. Der Blick geht über die rechte Schulter nach oben, die Arme ruhen auf den Oberschenkeln. Die Hände sind mit Handschuhen geschützt, in die kantige Lederriemen eingearbeitet sind – um die Wirkung des eigenen Schlages und damit das Verletzungsrisiko des Gegners zu erhöhen.

Im Gegensatz zum austrainierten und unverletzten, wenn auch blutver-
schmierten Körper des Sportlers (im Boxkampf der Antike durfte nur zum Kopf geschlagen werden, was dazu führte, dass Augen und Zähne oft brutal beschädigt wurden), zeugt sein Gesicht von vergangenen und aktuellen Kämpfen: Die Nase ist platt, als sei sie mindestens schon einmal gebrochen gewesen; die Augen liegen tief in den Höhlen, sind geschwollen; Wunden bluten. Um diesen Effekt zu verstärken, nutzte der Bildhauer »farbige Einlegearbeiten, die die schweren Verwundungen im Gesicht und an den Ohren, aber auch das vom Kopf auf Schultern, rechten Oberarm und rechten Oberschenkel herabtropfende Blut in Kupfer angeben. Ein Hämatom unter dem rechten Auge wurde in einer speziellen Bronzelegierung als separates Element gegossen und eingefügt.«[7] Für Edilberto Formigli ist die Statue gar das bis dato »einzige wissenschaftlich belegte Beispiel für eine Farbgebung durch die Anwendung von verschiedenartigen Legierungen«.[8]

Was der Künstler der Antike mit verschiedenfarbigen Metallen zu erreichen suchte, übersetzte der griechische Grammatiker und Dichter Lukillos von Tarrha, der sich in seinen Epigrammen besonders gern über Boxer ausließ, im ersten nachchristlichen Jahrhundert in einem Spott-
gedicht auf einen Kämpfer namens Stratophon in Verse:

»Als sich im zwanzigsten Jahr Odysseus nach Hause gerettet, / da erkannte sein Hund Argos ihn an der Gestalt. / Dich aber, Stratophon, nun, der du eben vier Stunden geboxt hast, / Kennen die Hunde zwar noch, aber kein Mensch mehr in der Stadt. / Geh nur, wenn's dich gelüstet, betrachte dein Antlitz im Spiegel, / Und du schwörst dann sofort: ›Nein, ich bin Stratophon nicht.‹«[9]

Es sind nicht die einzigen Zeilen, in denen der Dichter die brutalen Entstellungen schildert, die Faustkämpfer in der Antike kennzeichneten. In einem anderen Vers warnt er etwa einen Boxer, in Wasser mit spiegelglatter Oberfläche zu blicken – er würde vor Schreck sterben. Damit bildet Lukillos ebenso die Realität ab, wie der unbekannte Künstler, der den »Faustkämpfer vom Quirinal« schuf.

Runde 6 – Max Schmeling kauft sich einen Smoking und geht zu George Grosz

Ein anderer Vers entstand in den Zwanzigerjahren des vergangenen Jahrhunderts in Berlin. Will man dem Verfasser Glauben schenken, schrieb er den Zweizeiler aus einer Laune

Faustkämpfer, 2. Hälfte des 4. Jh. v. Chr. oder
3. Jh. v. Chr.
Boxer at Rest, 2nd half of the 4th century BCE
or 3rd century BCE

in antiquity. In another rhyme, for instance, he advises a boxer against looking into water with a perfectly smooth surface, as he would die from shock. Lucilius thus depicted reality just as the unknown artist did in creating the **Boxer at Rest**.

Round 6—Max Schmeling Buys Himself a Tuxedo and Goes to George Grosz

A different kind of verse was composed in Berlin in the 1920s. If the author is to be believed, he wrote the distich on a whim after attending a soirée at the gallery of the art dealer, Alfred Flechthcim (1878–1937):

Künstler, schenkt mir Eure Gunst, / Boxen ist doch auch 'ne Kunst. [Artists, bestow upon me your favor / For boxing, too, is an art you can savor.][10]

The rhyme may be clumsy and the punchline obvious, but nonetheless the entry Max Schmeling (1905–2005) wrote in the guest book of **the** German art dealer in Fauvism and Cubism documents the close relationship between intellectuals and artists on the one hand and boxers on the other—a relationship that, sometimes more intense and sometimes less, endured over time.

Contrary to what Schmeling suggests, the fascination was, in fact, mutual and it was not up to the athletes to compete for attention. Schmeling at the time bought himself a tuxedo and a dress coat—"two pieces of clothing that everybody was wearing by then, to the premiere as well as at the boxing ring."[11] During the Weimar Republic the sporting and cultural scenes were particularly closely linked. Only the excitement about the Berlin six-day race stood comparison with public interest in boxing matches.

Rudolf Grossmann,
Die Boxer (The Boxers), 1921

heraus nach einer Soiree in den Räumen des Kunsthändlers Alfred Flechtheim (1878–1937):

»Künstler schenkt mir Eure Gunst / Boxen ist doch auch ’ne Kunst.«[10]

Der Reim mag holpern, die Pointe naheliegend sein – dennoch dokumentiert Max Schmeling (1905–2005) mit seinem Eintrag im Gästebuch **des** deutschen Kunsthändlers des Fauvismus und Kubismus die enge Verbindung zwischen Intellektuellen und Künstlern auf der einen Seite sowie Faustkämpfern auf der anderen Seite. Eine Beziehung, die durch die Zeitläufte Bestand hatte, mal intensiver, mal laxer gelebt wurde.

Dabei war es keineswegs wie von Schmeling suggeriert: Die Faszination war tatsächlich gegenseitig, es lag nicht an den Sportlern, um Aufmerksamkeit buhlen zu müssen. Schmeling hat sich seinerzeit erstmals Frack und Smoking gekauft – »zwei Kleidungsstücke, die inzwischen jedermann trug, in der Premiere wie am Boxring«.[11] In der Weimarer Republik

waren Sport- und Kulturszene besonders eng verknüpft. Nur die Begeisterung fürs Berliner Sechstagerennen hielt dem Vergleich mit dem Publikumsinteresse an Faustkämpfen stand.

Flechtheim notierte im Januar 1926 in seinem Kulturmagazin »Der Querschnitt«, für das auch Boxer schrieben und das dazu beitrug, den Sport intellektuell-ästhetisch zu diskutieren, folgende Boobachtung anlässlich des Schwergewichtkampfes zwischen Hans Breitensträter (1897–1972) und dem Spanier Paolino Uzcudun (1899–1985): »[...] das Publikum [...] rekrutiert sich nicht allein aus Bierkutschern und Chauffeuren; die ganze gute berlinische Gesellschaft ist da, Prinzen und Prinzessinnen, Maler und Bildhauer, Literatur und Haute Banque und alle an diesem Abend beschäftigungslosen Schauspieler.«[12] Die 15 000 Plätze im Berliner Sportpalast waren 1925 bereits acht Tage vor dem Ereignis ausverkauft. Obwohl Uzcudun durch Knockout gewonnen hatte, entstand Deutschlands erster Sport-Dokumentarfilm. Adolf Abter führte Regie bei **Breitensträter –**

Paolino. Des deutschen Meisters schwerster Kampf.

Schon 1921 hatte Flechtheim die Mappe **Boxer** des Malers und Grafikers Rudolf Grossmann mit acht handkolorierten Lithografien herausgegeben, zu der Breitensträter das Vorwort verfasste. Fortan wurde der Schwergewichtler als Mitarbeiter des »Querschnitts« geführt, das Blatt nannte sich seit seiner Gründung im Jahr 1921 im Untertitel »Magazin für Literatur, Kunst und Boxsport«. Die Darstellung des Faustkampfs in diesem Heft »konfrontierte Sport und Kunst miteinander und hob darüber hinaus den Sport selbst in den Rang einer Kunst«.[13]

Doch zurück zu Schmeling, der inzwischen einen Smoking besaß und auf den Festen Flechtheims, der ihn im Übrigen zu überzeugen versuchte, Picasso zu sammeln, als »Paradestück«[14] galt. Mehr noch. Der Schwergewichtler war in den Zwanzigerjahren Modell für diverse Künstler. Wie der Boxer muss auch der Maler bei einer Porträtsitzung sein Gegenüber taxieren, einschätzen, erfassen.

George Grosz, *Max Schmeling der Boxer
(Max Schmeling the Boxer)*, 1926

In the January 1926 issue of his cultural magazine **Der Querschnitt**, which counted boxers among its contributors and helped create an intellectual and aesthetic discourse on the sport, Flechtheim noted the following observation on the occasion of the heavyweight fight between Hans Breitensträter (1897–1972) and the Spaniard Paolino Uzcudun (1899–1985): "[…] The audience […] is not just made up of beer delivery drivers and chauffeurs; all of Berlin high society is there; princes and princesses, painters and sculptors, writers and major bankers and all the actors who are not employed this evening."[12] The 15,000 seats at the Berlin Sportpalast were sold out eight days before the 1925 event. Even though Uzcudun won by a knockout, the fight yielded the first German sports documentary: **Breitensträter – Paolino. Des deutschen Meisters schwerster Kampf** [Breitensträter – Paolino. The German Champion's Toughest Fight], directed by Adolf Abter.

As early as 1921, Flechtheim had published a portfolio of eight hand-colored lithographs by the painter and graphic artist, Rudolf Grossmann; titled **Boxer**, it included a foreword by Breitensträter. From then on the heavyweight was listed as a contributor to **Querschnitt.** Ever since it had been launched in 1921 the periodical's subtitle read "Magazine for literature, art and boxing." The portrayal of pugilism in this issue "confronted sport and art with one another and, what is more, elevated the sport itself to the rank of a fine art."[13]

But let us return to Schmeling, who by now owned a tuxedo and was considered a "big draw" at the parties of Flechtheim who, incidentally, tried to persuade him to collect the work of Picasso.[14] Moreover, the heavyweight sat for various artists in the 1920s. Like a boxer, the painter, too, must size up, assess, and appreciate the person across from him at a portrait session. He must work with him without knowing him and must find access to the unfamiliar body. Artists

Er muss mit ihm arbeiten, ohne ihn zu kennen; muss einen Zugang zu dem ihm unbekannten Körper finden. Künstler wie Sportler müssen den anderen begreifen, ihn »lesen« lernen, um ihn malen oder treffen zu können. In seiner Autobiografie erinnert sich Schmeling: »[…] die Künstler der Zeit zwischen den Kriegen von George Grosz über Rudolf Belling und Renée Sintenis bis Ernesto de Fiori malten und modellierten mich.«[15] Vor allem mit den Werken von Grosz (1893–1959) tat sich der Sportler jedoch schwer, das meiste habe ihn abgestoßen.[16]

Dennoch ließ er sich von ihm in dessen Atelier an der Nassauischen Straße porträtieren. Grosz, berichtet Schmeling, habe ihn überrascht mit der Aussage, er wolle ihn als »Typus des Faustkämpfers« malen, als »Idee des Mannes im Ring«. Das laute Geräusch des Pinsels verunsicherte den Boxer während der Sitzungen zusätzlich: »Ein wenig war ich nun doch besorgt, denn die vehemente Art, in der Grosz die Leinwand traktierte, ließ mich befürchten, er werde auch aus mir einen jener rüden rücksichts-

losen Zeit-Typen machen, die mich bei Flechtheim so befremdet hatten.«[17] Doch die beiden schienen Gemeinsamkeiten entdeckt und sich prächtig unterhalten zu haben – etwa darüber, dass im Ring Intelligenz wichtig ist. Auf Schmelings Hinweis, ein physisch scheinbar schwächerer Boxer könne viel mit »Taktik und Strategie« wettmachen, habe Grosz geantwortet: »Auch beim Maler kommt es ja nicht auf den größten Tuschkasten an.«[18]

Als das Ölgemälde 1926 fertig war – in jenem August wurde Schmeling durch einen K.-o.-Sieg gegen Max Diekmann Deutscher Meister im Halbschwergewicht – waren alle zufrieden: der Maler, der Galerist – und auch der Porträtierte war »angetan und natürlich ein wenig geschmeichelt, vom umstrittenen George Grosz verewigt worden zu sein«.[19] Das Bild, das ein Bekannter Schmelings nach dem Krieg dessen langjährigem Freund, dem Verleger Axel Springer schenkte, zeigt den Sportler in einer eher ungewöhnlichen Kampfpose, beide Fäuste vor dem Bauch. Auffallend ist, dass Grosz den Athleten in

der Bewegung von rechts nach links gemalt hat: In der Bildwirkung löst das, da es konträr zur Leserichtung ist, Widerstand beim Betrachter aus – sehr elegant vermittelt die Arbeit auf diese Weise die große Anstrengung des Boxens.

Runde 7 – Brecht, der Box-Dialektiker

Von jener Anstrengung freilich wollte Bertolt Brecht (1898–1956) nichts wissen in seinem Libretto für Kurt Weills Oper **Aufstieg und Fall der Stadt Mahagonny**, die 1930 uraufgeführt wurde. Darin heißt es:

»Erstens, vergeßt nicht, kommt das Fressen / Zweitens kommt der Liebesakt / Drittens das Boxen nicht vergessen / Viertens Saufen, laut Kontrakt / Vor allem aber achtet scharf / Daß man hier alles dürfen darf.«[20]

Brecht treibt die Stimmung der Zeit auf die Spitze und überhöht den Boxsport zum menschlichen Grundbedürfnis, dessen Erfüllung unmittelbar nach Nahrung und Fortpflanzung

Gerald Brettschuh,
Box-Comic, 1977

as well as athletes must understand the other, learn to "read" him, in order to be able to paint or hit him. As Schmeling remembers in his autobiography: "[…] The artists of the interwar period, from George Grosz and Rudolf Belling to Renée Sintenis and Ernesto de Fiori, painted and modeled me."[15] Still, the athlete had a hard time especially with the works of Grosz (1893–1959), most of which he found repellent.[16]

Nonetheless he had Grosz paint his portrait at his studio on Nassauische Strasse. According to Schmeling's account, the artist surprised him by stating he wanted to paint him as the "boxer type," as the "idea of a man in the ring." The loud noise of the brush additionally unnerved the boxer during the sessions: "I did worry a bit now, as the harsh way in which Grosz treated the canvas made me fear that he would turn me into one of those uncouth, ruthless types of the time that had already disconcerted me at Flechtheim's."[17] Still, the two apparently discovered they had things in common and had a splendid

time talking to each other, about how important intelligence is in the ring, for instance. When Schmeling pointed out that a physically apparently weaker boxer could to a large extent make up for this with "tactics and strategy," Grosz was said to have answered: "For a painter, too, it is not about the biggest paint box."[18]

When Grosz's oil painting was finished in 1926—in August of the same year Schmeling won the German light heavyweight championship after a knockout victory over Max Diekmann—everybody was happy: the painter, the art dealer, and the sitter too felt "pleased and, of course, somewhat flattered to have been immortalized by the controversial George Grosz."[19] The painting, which an acquaintance of Schmeling gave to the latter's long-standing friend, the publisher Axel Springer, after the war, shows the athlete in an unusual fighting stance with both fists in front of his abdomen. Strikingly, Grosz painted him moving from right to left, which, in terms of visual effect, causes resistance in the viewer, be-

cause it is contrary to the direction of reading. In this way the work very elegantly conveys the great effort involved in boxing.

Round 7—Brecht, the Dialectician of Boxing

Bertolt Brecht (1898–1956), on the other hand, would have none of this effort in his score for Kurt Weill's opera **Rise and Fall of the City of Mahagonny**, which premiered in 1930. There we read:

First, remember, comes stuffing yourself / Second comes the act of love / Thirdly / don't forget the boxing / Fourthly boozing, as per contract / But above all remember this / That here you can do whatever you like.[20]

Brecht takes the mood of the day to extremes and elevates boxing to a basic human need whose fulfillment is to come right after nourishment and procreation. The author sees boxing as synonymous with the distraction and pleasure addiction of man, linked in **Mahagonny** with gambling. At the

kommen muss. Für den Autor ist der Faustkampf Synonym für Zerstreuung und Vergnügungssucht des Menschen, in Mahagonny verbunden mit dem Glücksspiel. Zugleich wehrte er sich in den Zwanzigerjahren mehrfach gegen Versuche, den Sport zur Kunst zu erklären, und griff zugleich kaum verhohlen Flechtheims »Querschnitt« an: »Neben James Joyce prangte Herr Diener [Franz Diener, 1901–1969, deutscher Schwergewichtler; Anm. d. Autors]. Ist es bösartig anzunehmen, daß diese Zeitschrift damit eher Herrn Diener als Herrn Joyce nützen wollte?«[21] Brecht überschrieb diesen Artikel, der 1928 in dem von Willy Meisl herausgegebenen Buch **Der Sport am Scheideweg** erstmals erschien, mit »Die Krise des Sportes« und argumentierte heftig gegen die Verquickung von Boxen und Kultur – »schon dar-

um, weil ich weiß, was diese Gesellschaft mit Kulturgütern alles treibt, und der Sport dazu wirklich zu schade ist. Ich bin für den Sport, weil und solange er riskant (ungesund), unkultiviert (also nicht gesellschaftsfähig) und Selbstzweck ist.«[22]

Natürlich hielt jedoch seine vehemente Kritik etwa am Punktesystem zur Ermittlung des Siegers in Kämpfen ohne K. o. den leidenschaftlichen Dialektiker nicht davon ab, selbst über das Boxen zu schreiben – und mit diesen Texten Geld zu verdienen. So arbeitete der Autor mit Paul Samson-Körner (1887–1942) an dessen Biografie, die 1926 als Fortsetzungsgeschichte zunächst im Berliner »Scherl's Magazin« erschien, wo Brecht auch die Boxer-Kurzgeschichte **Der Kinnhaken** veröffentlichte. Später wurde sie in der Sportzeitschrift »Die

Arena« weitergeführt. Brecht brachte den Lebensbericht des Sportlers in eine literarische Form, der 1908 aus seiner Geburtsstadt Zwickau in die USA ausgewandert war und dort das Boxen gelernt hatte. Sportler-Biografien seien eine »reizvolle Herausforderung für jeden Schriftsteller«, wie Elio Menéndez und Victor Joaquín Ortega zu Beginn ihres Buchs über den Kubaner »Kid Chocolate« schreiben – ähnlich mag es Brecht mit Samson-Körners Vita ergangen sein. Wie viele seiner Kollegen war der Autor fasziniert vom allegorischen Potenzial des Boxens, von der Grenzerfahrung vor allem im Moment des Knockouts. Daher auch seine bereits erwähnte Ablehnung des Punktesystems. »Je weiter sich der Boxsport vom K. o. entfernt, desto weniger hat er mit wirklichem Sport zu tun. Ein Boxer,

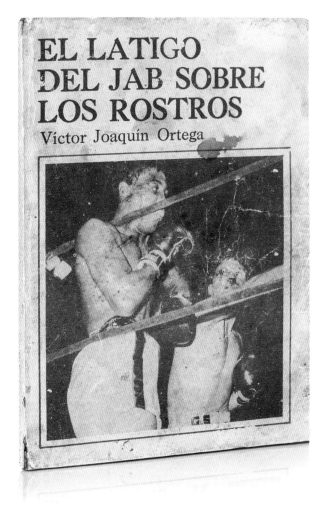

Victor Joaquin Ortega, *El látigo del jab sobre los rostros. Novela testimonio*, Editora Abril de la UJC, 1986

— **Kunst und K.o.**

same time he objected on a number of occasions to attempts to proclaim the sport an art. He also unleashed an ill-concealed attack against Flechtheim's **Querschnitt**: "Alongside James Joyce it shows Mr. Diener [Franz Diener, 1901–69, German heavyweight; author's note]. Is it malicious to assume that, in doing so, this magazine wanted to help Mr. Diener rather than Mr. Joyce?"[21] First published in **Der Sport am Scheideweg** [Sport at the Crossroads], a 1928 collection of essays edited by Willy Meisl, Brecht titled his article "The Crisis of Sport" and argued vehemently against the intertwining of boxing and culture: "If only because I know what this society is doing with cultural assets, and the sport is just too good for that. I am a proponent of the sport, because and as long as it is dangerous (unhealthy), uncultivated (i.e., not socially acceptable) and an end in itself."[22]

Yet, of course, his fierce criticism—for instance, of the point system used to determine the winner in fights without a knockout—did not keep the passionate dialectician from writing about boxing himself and making money from those texts. Thus he worked with Paul Samson-Körner (1887–1942) on the biography of this German heavyweight boxer, which was initially serialized in the Berlin-based **Scherl's Magazin** in 1926, where Brecht also published a short story about a boxer called "Der Kinnhaken" [The Uppercut]. The biography was subsequently continued in the sports magazine **Die Arena**. Brecht put the story of the athlete, who in 1908 had left his native city of Zwickau to move to the USA where he learned to box, into literary form. Athlete biographies are an "exciting challenge for any writer," as Elio Menéndez and Victor Joaquín Ortega write at the beginning of their book on Cuba's Kid Chocolate, and Brecht may have felt the same about his biography of Samson-Körner. Like many of his fellow writers, the author was fascinated by the allegorical potential of boxing, by the borderline experience especially in the knockout moment—hence his aforementioned rejection of the point system. "The further boxing moves away from the knockout, the less it has to do with real sport. A boxer who cannot knock down his opponent has certainly not defeated him."[23]

These words are somewhat reminiscent of Billy Ray, whose business card introduced him as the "Last Surviving Bare-Knuckle Fighter." To A.J. Liebling's question of how many fights he had been in, Ray responded shortly before his ninetieth birthday: "A hundred forty. The last one was with gloves. I thought the game was getting soft, so I retired."[24] The Queensberry rules, the basis of modern boxing, became widely accepted by the end of the 19th century. With that the era of bare-knuckle fights was officially over.

Round 8—On Loneliness, in the Ring and at the Writing Desk

With or without gloves, boxing fascinates the literati. Numerous authors have slogged away at this sport and its protagonists like a challenger at

Kid Chocolate

der seinen Gegner nicht niederschlagen kann, hat ihn natürlich nicht besiegt.«[23]

Ein bisschen erinnern diese Zeilen an Billy Ray, dessen Visitenkarte ihn wie folgt vorstellte: »Letzter überlebender Vertreter des Boxkampfes mit bloßen Fäusten«. Auf A. J. Lieblings Frage, wie oft er gekämpft habe, antwortete Ray kurz vor seinem 90. Geburtstag: »Hundertvierzigmal. Das letzte Mal mit Handschuhen. Da hab ich gedacht: Der Sport wird schlapp, und hab aufgehört.«[24] Die Queensberry-Regeln, Grundlage des modernen Boxsports, setzten sich Ende des 19. Jahrhunderts durch. Die Ära der Bareknuckle-Kämpfe war damit offiziell zu Ende.

Runde 8 – von der Einsamkeit, im Ring und am Schreibtisch

Ob mit oder ohne Handschuhe: Boxen fasziniert Literaten. Zahlreiche Autoren arbeiten sich an diesem Sport und seinen Protagonisten ab wie ein Herausforderer auf dem Weg zum lang ersehnten Titelkampf am Sandsack. Rund 150 Romane und Erzählungen, schätzt der Literaturwissenschaftler Manfred Luckas, der über »Mythen des Boxens und ihre literarische Inszenierung« promovierte, drehen sich um den Faustkampf.[25] Das ist jedoch nur der Blick ins innerste Zentrum des Rings.

Da ist etwa Vladimir Nabokov (1899–1977), der sich in seiner Autobiografie **Erinnerung sprich** (1967) an die Bibliothek seines Elternhauses in St. Petersburg erinnert, in der das Leder der Boxhandschuhe und jenes der Bucheinbände vereint gewesen seien. Da ist natürlich der große Box- und Kuba-Fan Ernest Hemingway (1899–1961), der es in Sachen Selbstbewusstsein noch mit jedem Profi aufnehmen konnte und seine Schriftsteller-Vita daher in der Sprache des Sports vortrug: »Ich fing ganz leise an und schlug Mr. Turgenjew. Dann ging ich hart ins Training und schlug Mr. de Maupassant. Mit Mr. Stendhal hatte ich zwei Unentschieden. Aber keiner kriegt mich je in den Ring mit Mr. Tolstoi, falls ich nicht närrisch werde oder mich noch sehr verbessere.«[26] Da ist George Bernard Shaw (1856–1950), der wie Hemingway selbst boxte und einen Faustkämpfer zur Hauptfigur seines Romans **Cashel Byron's Profession** (1882) machte. Boxbegeistert war auch **Sherlock Holmes**-Erfinder Sir Arthur Conan Doyle (1859–1930). Und da ist natürlich der bereits genannte Jack London, für den das Boxen literarisches und journalistisches Sujet war. Selbiges gilt für Wolf Wondratschek, Jahrgang 1943, der im TV-Gespräch mit Alexander Kluge jedoch Wert auf die Feststellung legt, dass er seine Boxreportagen nie als Sportreportagen begriffen habe: »Über den Sport kann man ja nicht so viel erzählen. Es sind Reportagen aus der Dritten Welt. Es ist das Subproletariat, aus dem die Weltmeister kommen.«[27] Damit liefert er nebenbei auch eine Erklärung für die Boxbegeisterung der Kubaner.

Nicht zuletzt sind es die Verlierer, die Autoren wie Wondratschek interessieren. Schriftsteller, schreibt er, »lieben die Geschundenen und Erledigten – vielleicht aus dem Grund nur, weil sie die besseren Geschichten abgeben. [...] Was alle schwächt, macht die Story stark. Sie [die Autoren; Anm. d. Autors] nehmen den Glanz noch von jenen, die ins Dunkel stürzen. [...] Wo Sieger feiern, sind sie Partygäste. Wenn sie fallen, beginnt ihr Job. Und doch ist der Schriftsteller der einzige Bruder des Boxers, der Verbündete seiner Einsamkeit.«[28]

Ähnlich sah das A. J. Liebling ein halbes Jahrhundert früher: »Ein Boxer

the punching bag on the way to a long-awaited title fight. About 150 novels and stories deal with boxing, according to Manfred Luckas, a literary scholar who wrote his dissertation on "Myths of Boxing and their Literary Mise-en-Scène."[25] But that is just a look at the innermost center of the ring.

There is, for example, Vladimir Nabokov (1899–1977) who in his 1967 autobiography **Speak, Memory** remembers the library of his family home in Saint Petersburg, where the leather of boxing gloves and that of book covers were united. And then there is, of course, the big fan of boxing and Cuba, Ernest Hemingway (1899–1961), who could hold his own against any pro as far as self-confidence was concerned, and who would therefore recite his résumé as a writer in the idiom of boxing: "I started out very quiet and I beat Mr. Turgenev. Then I trained hard and I beat Mr. de Maupassant. I've fought two draws with Mr. Stendhal, and I think I had an edge in the last one. But nobody's going to get me in any ring with Mr. Tolstoy, unless I'm crazy or I keep getting better."[26] There is George Bernard Shaw (1856–1950), like Hemingway a boxer himself, who made a pugilist the protagonist of his 1882 novel **Cashel Byron's Profession**. And the creator of Sherlock Holmes, Sir Arthur Conan Doyle (1859–1930), was a boxing enthusiast

as well. And then there is, of course, the aforementioned Jack London for whom boxing was both a literary and a journalistic subject. The same is true of German writer Wolf Wondratschek (b. 1943), although he has insisted in a TV interview with Alexander Kluge that he never thought of his boxing coverage as sports reporting: "There is not that much to tell about the sport. The stories are reports from the Third World. The sub-proletariat is where the world champions come from."[27] With this he incidentally also provided an explanation for the boxing enthusiasm of the Cubans.

Often the losers, too, are of interest to authors such as Wondratschek. Writers, he notes, "love the mauled and the washed-up—if only because they provide the better stories. [...] That which weakens everybody makes the story strong. They [the writers; author's note] take the luster even of those who are plunging into darkness. [...] Where winners celebrate, they are party guests. When they fall, their job begins. And yet the writer is the only brother of the boxer, the ally of his loneliness."[28]

Half a century earlier, A.J. Liebling offered a similar view: "A boxer, like a writer, must stand alone. If he loses he cannot call an executive conference and throw off on a vice president or the assistant sales manager. He is consequently resented by fractional characters who cannot live outside an organization."[29]

Similarly evoked by Norman Mailer (1923–2007), the pleasure in loneliness is certainly one reason for the love so many authors have for boxing. Yet aside from the machismo and self-dramatization of writers there are also dramaturgical arguments. Joyce Carol Oates explains the fascination boxing exerts on authors (herself included) by the fact that it is a "spectacle, in itself wordless, lacking a language, that requires others to define it, celebrate it, complete it."[30] Moreover, the illuminated square of a boxing ring is obviously reminiscent of theater. Boxing is concentrated drama, and therefore close to Aristotle's definition of tragedy as an "imitation of an action that is serious and also, as having magnitude, complete in itself."[31] For anything is possible in the 2,160 seconds a twelve-round fight lasts: a hero's fall and resurrection.

Round 9—The Big Toe of God

One boxer who, through alternating ascents and downfalls, rose to become the "Greatest of all Time" has long been an icon of pop culture. Muhammad Ali's name is found in the everyday realms of advertising and consumption as well as in literature, the visual arts, photography, and film. Michael Mann brought the life of the heavyweight boxer to the screen with Will Smith in the title role. Ali is a **topos** of poetry and prose. Norman Mailer used the 1974 fight in Kinshasa, Zaire,

muss wie ein Autor alleine dastehen. Wenn er verliert, kann er keine Vorstandskonferenz einberufen und einen Vizepräsidenten oder den stellvertretenden Verkaufsdirektor fertigmachen. Deshalb mögen ihn die kleinen Charaktere nicht, die außerhalb einer Organisation gar nicht existieren können.«[29]

Die Lust an der Einsamkeit, die auch Norman Mailer (1923–2007) beschwor, ist sicher ein Grund für die Faustkampf-Liebe derart vieler Autoren. Doch neben Machismo und Selbstinszenierung der Schriftsteller gibt es dramaturgische Argumente. Joyce Carol Oates erklärt die Faszination, die das Boxen auf Autoren (einschließlich ihrer selbst) ausübt, mit der Tatsache, dass es »ein Schauspiel ohne Worte ist, sprachlos, dass es andere braucht, die es in Worte fassen, die seine Triumphe besingen, es vervollkommnen«.[30] Außerdem erinnert das beleuchtete Geviert eines Rings natürlich an ein Theater. Boxen ist konzentrierte Dramatik – und damit nah dran an Aristoteles' Definition der Tragödie, einer »guten und in sich geschlossenen Handlung von bestimmter Größe«.[31] Denn alles ist möglich in jenen 2160 Sekunden, die ein Kampf über zwölf Runden dauert: Heldensturz und Auferstehung.

Runde 9 – der große Zeh Gottes
Ein Boxer, der über dem Wechselspiel von Aufstieg und Niedergang zum »Greatest of all Time« avancierte, ist längst Ikone der Popkultur. Muhammad Alis Name findet sich in den Alltäglichkeiten von Werbung und Konsum ebenso wie in Literatur, bildender Kunst, Fotografie und Film. Michael Mann brachte mit Will Smith in der Titelrolle das Leben des Schwergewichtlers auf die Leinwand. Ali ist Topos von Lyrik und Prosa. Norman Mailer nutzte den als »Rumble in the Jungle« berühmt gewordenen Kampf zwischen dem Weltmeister George Foreman und seinem Herausforderer Ali 1974 in Kinshasa, Zaire, für eine Demonstration in Sachen »New Journalism«, subjektiv und satt an Assoziationen. So spannend wie kurios ist ein Beitrag Mailers, der drei Jahre zuvor im US-Magazin »Life« über den »Fight of the Century« zwischen Weltmeister Joe Frazier und Ali erschienen war. Der Kampf im März 1971 im New Yorker Madison Square Garden, den Frazier für sich entschied, war Auftakt einer langjährigen Rivalität der beiden Boxer, die 1975 im »Thrilla in Manila« gipfelte. In seinem mit »Ego« überschriebenen »Life«-Artikel charakterisiert Mailer Ali als »the very spirit of the 20th Century, he is the prince of mass man and the media«[32] – wohl

kaum ahnend, wie recht er damit behalten sollte. Zudem findet der Autor wuchtige Formulierungen, um seine Faszination halbwegs in Sätze zwingen zu können. Diese, gelesen aus heutiger Perspektive, künden in ihrem Pathos freilich eher von Hilflosigkeit: »So, two great fighters in a great fight travel down subterranean rivers of exhaustion and cross mountain peaks of agony, stare at the light of their own death in the eye of the man they are fighting, travel into the crossroads of the most excruciating choice of karma as they get up from the floor against all the appeal of the sweet swooming catacombs of oblivion.«[33] Nur folgerichtig ist in diesem Fall, wenn Mailer in den (zumindest von ihm imaginierten) Gefühlshaushalt eines Weltmeisters blickt und bemerkt: »It is like being the big toe of God.«[34]

War man als Schwergewichts-Champion im Jahr 1971 Gottes großer Zeh, überrascht es nicht, dass der DC-Verlag sieben Jahre später Muhammad Ali mit und gegen seinen bekanntesten Superhelden antreten ließ: Neal Adams textete und zeichnete den Comic **Superman vs. Muhammad Ali.**

Runde 10 – gezeichnete Kämpfer
Muhammad Ali hat es im Comic zwar an die Seite des ersten und berühmtesten Superhelden geschafft. Doch

Ernest Hemingway als Boxer, 1944
Ernest Hemingway as boxer, 1944

that pitted world champion George Foreman against challenger Ali—the famous "Rumble in the Jungle"—to demonstrate "New Journalism," subjective and replete with associations. One article by Mailer about the "Fight of the Century" between Joe Frazier, the world champion, and Ali, which appeared three years earlier in **Life** magazine, is as gripping as it is curious. Won by Frazier, the March 1971 fight at Madison Square Garden in New York was the beginning of a longtime rivalry between the two boxers that culminated in the 1975 "Thrilla in Manila." In his **Life** article, which was titled "Ego," Mailer described Ali as "the very spirit of the 20th century, he is the prince of mass man and the media,"[32] hardly suspecting how right he would end up being. In addition, the author came up with grandiloquent verbalizations to be able to—at least to a certain extent—contain his fascination in sentences. Yet when read from today's perspective, his pathos bespeaks, if anything, helplessness: "So, two great fighters in a great fight travel down subterranean rivers of exhaustion and cross mountain peaks of agony, stare at the light of their own death in the eye of the man they are fighting, travel into the crossroads of the most excruciating choice of karma as they get up from

the floor against all the appeal of the sweet swooning catacombs of oblivion."[33] It is, in this case, only logical that when Mailer looks into the emotional state of mind of a world champion (at least as he imagines it) he finds: "It is like being the big toe of God."[34]

Having been the big toe of God as heavyweight champion in 1971, it is not surprising that, seven years later, DC Comics had Muhammad Ali fight alongside and against its most famous super hero: Neal Adams wrote and drew the comic book **Superman vs. Muhammad Ali**.

Round 10—Scarred Fighters

Muhammad Ali may have drawn level with the first and most famous superhero in comics, but this original genre of the "ninth art" has, in turn, inspired the international boxing circus and its athletes as well: on their ring walk few well-known athletes nowadays will refrain from wearing a splendid robe that they seem to have pulled off the shoulders of a superhero. In the study of comics the combat dress, usually completed by a cape and a mask, is considered to be a defining feature of those heroes who are modern versions of Greek or Nordic gods:[35]

dieses originäre Genre der »Neunten Kunst« hat auch den internationalen Boxzirkus und seine Sportler inspiriert: Kaum ein bekannter Athlet verzichtet heute beim Walk-In auf einen prachtvollen Mantel, den er einem Superhelden von den Schultern gerissen zu haben scheint. Der Kampfanzug, meist vervollständigt durch Umhang und Maske, gilt in der Comicforschung als Definitionsmerkmal jener Helden, die moderne Varianten griechischer oder nordischer Götter sind:[35] Superman, Batman, Green Lantern und Wonder Woman tragen solche Umhänge – und dürfen daher zumindest modisch als Vorbilder für die Profiboxer gelten.[36]

Erzählt die grafische Literatur vom Faustkampf selbst, orientiert sie sich an einer Bildsprache, die das Kino etabliert hat – oder sie macht sich über den angeblich tumben Sport lustig. Im Album **Asterix bei den Olympischen Spielen** (1968), dem zwölften Band der Reihe um die unbeugsamen Gallier, zeichnete Albert Uderzo den Faustkämpfer Walros, genannt »Koloß von Rhodos«,[37] als Fleischberg mit einem Oberkörper wie ein Schrank. Im Verhältnis ist der Kopf des Sportlers klein; Hasenzähne verstärken den dämlichen Eindruck dieses zwar bärenstarken, doch harmlos-naiven Zeitgenossen.

Mit ähnlichen Merkmalen arbeitete der spanische Zeichner Juanjo Guarnido in der Serie **Blacksad** (2000). Zusammen mit dem Szenaristen Juan Díaz Canales erzählt er im Stil des Film noir eine Detektivgeschichte, in der alle Protagonisten vermenschlichte Tiere sind. Der ehemalige Leibwächter der Ermordeten ist Boxer; Guarnido zeichnete ihn als massigen Gorilla, der im Kampf erstaunlich beweglich ist. Im Gespräch jenseits des Rings zeigen Szenarist und Zeichner ihn als Großmaul, das zwar das Herz am rechten Fleck zu haben scheint, das jedoch – siehe **Asterix bei den Olympischen Spielen** – nicht sonderlich helle ist: »Das Gedächtnis war immer mein Schwachpunkt.«[38]

Solch klischeehafte Darstellungen finden sich genreunabhängig vor allem bei Nebenfiguren. Es gibt aber auch Zeichner, die das Boxen geschickt als Metapher nutzen. So erzählt der Franzose Alfred in **Come Prima** (2013) die Geschichte zweier ungleicher Brüder in den Fünfzigerjahren; der eine hält sich als Boxer mehr schlecht als recht über Wasser. Auf den ersten Seiten des Buchs, das 2014 beim bedeutenden Comicfestival in Angoulême als »Album des Jahres« ausgezeichnet wurde, verwebt Alfred feinfühlig Szenen eines Boxkampfes mit dem Augenblick, in dem sich die Brüder

nach vielen Jahren wiedersehen: Das Boxen steht hier stellvertretend für den Kampf mit der Familie als auch für den gegen die eigenen Dämonen.

Beide Gegner kennt Anton Witkowski, Hauptfigur in **Wut im Bauch** (2004/06). Der Franzose Hervé Barulea, der seine Arbeiten als Baru signiert, schildert Witkowskis Geschichte mit farbsattem Strich. In dem zweibändigen Album finden sich ebenso wie in Barus **Der Champion** (1990) Motive, die aus Boxfilmen bekannt sind: Das letztgenannte Buch handelt von einem algerischen Boxer in den letzten Jahren der französischen Kolonialherrschaft. Im Zentrum von **Wut im Bauch** steht ein junger polnischstämmiger Kämpfer, der sich aus der Banlieue von Paris bis zur Weltmeisterschaft boxt – trotz seiner Herkunft und gegen den Willen seiner Eltern. Sein härtester Gegner dabei ist jedoch der eigene Jähzorn, der ihn letztlich vor Gericht bringt.

Während Baru mit Vorliebe Zeithistorie in (fiktiven) Bildromanen thematisiert, hat der deutsche Künstler Reinhard Kleist eine wahre Geschichte in die Sprache des Comics übersetzt: Seine 2012 erschienene Graphic Novel **Der Boxer** basiert auf der Vita des jüdischen Faustkämpfers Hertzko Haft (1925–2007), der die nationalsozialistischen Konzentrationslager nur über-

Joyce Carol Oates

Superman, Batman, Green Lantern, and Wonder Woman wear such robes and therefore can be regarded as role models, at least in terms of fashion, for professional boxers.[36]

When graphic novels tell stories about boxing itself, they tend to draw on the visual language established by the movies as a model—or, alternatively, they poke fun at the allegedly dumb sport. In **Asterix at the Olympic Games** (1968), the twelfth comic book album in the series about the indomitable Gauls, Albert Uderzo drew the pugilist Neuroses a.k.a. the "Colossus of Rhodes"[37] as a mountain of meat with a hulky torso. The athlete's head is small in comparison and buckteeth reinforce the dimwitted appearance of this strapping yet harmless and naïve fellow.

The Spanish comic artist, Juanjo Guarnido, worked with similar features in the comic album series **Blacksad** (2000). Together with writer Juan Díaz Canales, he tells a mystery story in **film noir** style. Its protagonists are all humanized animals and the former bodyguard of the murdered woman is a boxer. Guarnido draws him as a hulking great gorilla who is amazingly nimble in a fight. When talking outside of the ring, the writer and the illustrator depict him as a loudmouth who seems to have his heart in the right place, but is not particularly bright (see

Asterix at the Olympic Games): "Memory ain't one of my stronger points."[38]

Such stereotypical portrayals are found especially in minor characters, regardless of the genre. But there are also comic artists who skillfully use boxing as a metaphor. In the 2013 comic album **Come Prima**, the Frenchman Alfred tells the story of two very different brothers in the 1950s. One barely stays afloat as a boxer. On the first pages of the book, which won Best Album at the major comic festival in Angoulême in 2014, Alfred subtly interweaves scenes of a boxing match with the moment when the brothers meet again after many years: boxing here is a metaphor for the battle against one's family as well as for fighting one's own demons.

Both enemies are familiar to Anton Witkowski, the main character in the comic album series **L'Enragé** [The

Enraged, 2004 and 2006]. The French artist Hervé Barulea, who signs his work "Baru," paints Witkowski's story with a color-saturated line. The two-volume album, as well as Baru's 1990 **The Champion**, include imagery familiar from boxing movies: the latter album is about an Algerian boxer during the last years of French colonial rule. **L'Enragé** revolves around a young fighter of Polish descent who boxes his way up from the Paris **banlieue** to become champion of the world, in spite of his background and against the will of his parents. His toughest opponent, however, is his own violent temper which, eventually, causes him to end up in court.

While Baru has a penchant for addressing recent history in (fictitious) graphic novels, the German comic artist Reinhard Kleist has translated

lebte, weil er zur Unterhaltung der Wachmannschaften boxte: »Hier ging es in der Regel um Leben und Tod – ein einziges sadistisches Spektakel«, wie der Sportjournalist Martin Krauß im Nachwort zu Kleists expressivem Schwarz-Weiß-Comic schreibt.[39] Nach dem Krieg wanderte Haft in die USA aus, wo er als Harry Haft 21 Profikämpfe bestreiten sollte – den letzten im Jahr 1949 gegen den späteren Weltmeister im Schwergewicht, Rocky Marciano.

Runde 11 – Joyce Carol Oates, die Frau am Ring

Meist sind es Männer, die das Geschehen im Ring zu Literatur kondensieren. Doch 1987 ist in den USA mit **On Boxing** ein Essay über den Sport erschienen, der seit damals mehrfach neu aufgelegt und übersetzt wurde. Zweifelsohne ist **Über Boxen** eines der besten, kenntnisreichsten Bücher über den Sport – geschrieben von der US-Amerikanerin Joyce Carol Oates, Jahrgang 1938, deren Vater sie einst als Kind mit zu Kämpfen nahm. Oates, die immer wieder als Kandidatin für den Literaturnobelpreis genannt wird, macht keinen Hehl aus ihrer Begeisterung für und ihr großes Wissen um den Faustkampf.

Zugleich gelingt es ihr jedoch – und das unterscheidet **Über Boxen** von vielen Texten ihrer männlichen Kollegen –, die eigene Faszination zu reflektieren. Ein Glücksfall, für die Literatur **und** das Boxen.

Es gebe keine »einfache Antwort« auf die Frage nach dem Grund ihres Interesses, schreibt sie: Boxen sei für sie weder Sport – es habe nichts »Spielerisches, nichts Helles, nichts Gefälliges an sich. [...] Man spielt Football, aber man **spielt** nicht Boxen.«[40] Es funktioniere aber auch nicht wirklich als Metapher. Das Leben mag dem Boxen in »vielen beunruhigenden Beziehungen« ähnlich sein. »Aber Boxen gleicht nur sich selbst.«[41] Obwohl Oates einen Kampf lesen und analysieren kann wie der Literaturwissenschaftler ein Drama, weiß sie um die Schwierigkeiten, »das wortlose Schauspiel in eine erzählerische Einheit zu fassen«.[42] Denn: »Boxen steht eindeutig dem Tanz oder der Musik näher als der Erzählkunst.«[43] Diese Demut mag in den Ohren ihrer männlichen Kollegen albern klingen – wer die Texte der US-Amerikanerin liest, wird allerdings verstehen.

Runde 12 – The Final Countdown

Die zurückliegenden Runden haben gezeigt, dass Literaten gerne hart an Pathos und Kitsch vorbeischrammen oder diese Grenze testosteronschwanger einreißen, wenn sie über Boxen schreiben. Schließlich lassen sich innerhalb des Rings viele Aspekte des Daseins in konzentrierter Form finden, wie selbst Joyce Carol Oates einräumt. Auch der Boxexperte John E. Oden, der sein Geld als Direktor eines Finanzunternehmens verdient hat, damit als kühler Kopf und strategischer Denker

gelten darf, hält fest: »I have always believed that boxing is a metaphor for life.«[44] Und, geben wir es zu, es ist ja auch ein derbes Vergnügen für jeden Autor, beim Schreiben austeilen zu dürfen wie der Weltmeister in den drei Champions-Runden vor Kampfende. Der Italiener Davide Enia etwa hat sich dieser Freude in seinem Debütroman ungeniert hingegeben – und damit manchen Leser gerührt. Seinen Helden, den jungen Davidù, der sich seinen Platz diesseits und jenseits der Ringseile im Palermo der Achtzigerjahre erst erarbeiten muss, lässt Enia in einem furios erzählten Boxfinale Sätze formulieren, die so bedeutungsschwer und zugleich so treffend sind wie ein ansatzlos geschlagener Jab: »Ich war im Zustand der Gnade dessen, der zerstört. [...] Linke. Linke. Rechte. Linke. Rechte. Linke. Linke. Ich hoffte, es würde niemals aufhören. Ich war so ruhig und heiter wie der Zorn Gottes.«[45]

Graciano Rocchigiani, einst Weltmeister im Supermittelgewicht und Halbschwergewicht, hat, wie kann es anders sein, für die Debatte indes wenig übrig: Pathos ist nicht sein Ding. Boxen als Kunstform? Quatsch! »Mann am Boden – jutet Jeföhl.«[46] Darum gehe es.

Und natürlich kann man es auch so sehen.

Währenddessen sind die Boxer in ihren Akademien auf Kuba längst wieder am Arbeiten. Jeder für sich und doch alle zusammen. Für die nächsten drei Minuten.

Noch eine Runde Ewigkeit.

a true story into the language of the comic: his 2012 graphic novel **Der Boxer** is based on the life of the Jewish boxer, Hertzko Haft (1925–2007), who only survived the Nazi concentration camps, because he boxed for the entertainment of the camp guards: "These were usually fights to the death—pure sadistic spectacle," as sports journalist Martin Krauss writes in his afterword to Kleist's expressive black-and-white comic album.[39] After the war, Haft emigrated to the US where, as Harry Haft, he would fight 21 professional matches—the final one in 1949 against the later world heavyweight champion, Rocky Marciano.

Round 11—Joyce Carol Oates, the Woman at the Ring

Usually it is men who distill what happens in the ring into literature. But in 1987 an essay titled "On Boxing" was published in the US that has since seen several reprints and a number of translations into other languages. "On Boxing" is, without doubt, one of the best, most knowledgeable books about the sport. It was written by American author Joyce Carol Oates (b. 1938) whose father once used to take her to fights. Often rumored as a contender for the Nobel Prize in Literature, Oates makes no secret of her enthusiasm for and her extensive knowledge of boxing.

At the same time, however, she manages to reflect upon her own fascination, which is what distinguishes "On Boxing" from many of her male colleagues' texts — a lucky break for literature **and** for boxing.

"It is too complex to answer," she writes in response to the question of why she is so interested. Boxing, to her, is not a sport: there is "nothing fundamentally playful about it; nothing that seems to belong to daylight, to pleasure. [...] One **plays** football, one doesn't **play** boxing."[40] Also, it doesn't really work as a metaphor: "Life is like boxing in many unsettling respects. But boxing is only like boxing."[41] Although Oates can read and analyze a fight like a literary scholar reads and analyzes a drama, she is aware of the difficulties of giving to "the wordless spectacle a narrative unity."[42] Because boxing, she says, "is more clearly akin to dance or music than narrative."[43] This humility may sound silly to her male counterparts, but those who read the American writer's texts will understand.

Round 12—The Final Countdown

The past rounds have shown that literary writers like to come within an inch of pathos and kitsch or, heavy on testosterone, break down this boundary when writing about boxing. After all, many aspects of life can be found in concentrated form within the ring, as even Joyce Carol Oates admits. Boxing expert John E. Oden, who made his money as director of a financial company and hence can be considered to be level-headed and a strategic thinker, notes: "I have always believed that boxing is a metaphor for life."[44] And, let's admit, it is great fun for any author to be allowed to deal blows while writing the way the world champion does in the three champion's rounds before the end of the fight. The Italian writer, Davide Enia, for instance, has unashamedly indulged in this fun in his debut novel and, in the process, moved many a reader. In a rousingly narrated boxing finale, Enia has his hero, the young Davidù, who still has to fight to secure his place inside and outside of the ring ropes in 1980s Palermo, speak sentences that are as fraught with meaning and at the same time as striking as a jab coming out of nowhere: "I was in the state of grace of one who wreaks havoc. [...] Left. Left. Right. Left. Right. Left. Left. I wanted it to never end. I was as calm and unruffled as the wrath of God."[45]

Meanwhile Graciano Rocchigiani, the one-time super-middleweight and light-heavyweight champion of the world, doesn't care much about the debate: pathos is not his thing. Boxing as an art form? Baloney! "Man down— good feeling" he says in his thick Berlin accent.[46] To him that's what it is about.

And, obviously, this is another way of looking at it.

In the meantime, the boxers at their academies in Cuba have long gone back to work. Each for themselves and yet all together. For the next three minutes.

Another round of eternity.

Porträt und Milieu. El Boxeo in La Habana
Zu den Fotografien von Katharina Alt

Petra Giloy-Hirtz

I

»Un nuevo dia«, zitiert das offizielle Organ des Comité Central del Partido Comunista de Cuba den amerikanischen Präsidenten Barack Obama bei seinem »historischen Besuch« aus seiner Pressekonferenz im **teatro** des Palacio de la Revolución am 21. März 2016. Vier Tage später ruft Mick Jagger den 500 000 jubelnden Menschen, die zum Konzert der Rolling Stones in die Ciudad Deportiva in Havanna geströmt sind, in Spanisch zu: »Wir wissen, dass es viele Jahre schwierig war, unsere Musik in Kuba zu hören. Aber jetzt sind wir hier und spielen. Ich denke, die Zeiten ändern sich endlich.« Kuba im Frühling: Raúl Castro reicht die Hand, da mag sein greiser Bruder Fidel weiterhin die Ziele der Revolution von 1959 beschwören. Welch ein Moment!

Kuba wird gleichwohl noch lange Kulisse sein für die Bilder, für die es berühmt und geliebt ist: Paläste und Villen, phänomenale Architekturen, historisierend bis kühn modern, oft nur mehr kollabierende Strukturen, abgeblätterte Überreste einer einst stolz glänzenden Zeit, die alten Autos in ihren großartigen Farben, **mágico, místico**, unzählige Male abgelichtet und in Prachtbänden versammelt: ein verführerisches, gleichwohl limitiertes visuelles Vokabular, das auf Nostalgie, Melancholie und den Zauber der Dekadenz setzt. Das Bild des Landes in der Fotografie kubanischer Künstler sieht anders aus, denkt man etwa an das Werk von Alberto Korda aus den 1950er- und 1960er-Jahren oder an José A. Figueroa. Fotografen der postrevolutionären Zeit von 1990 bis heute kommentieren oft sozial- und kulturkritisch jene kubanischen Stereotypen.[1]

Auch Malerei, Zeichnung, Skulptur, Installation oder Video der dortigen Kunstszene haben nichts von der Romantik des exotistischen Blicks. Sie setzen sich mit dem geschichtlichen, politischen, sozialen und kulturellen Kontext Kubas auseinander, mit Revolution, Flucht, Emigration, Zensur und Gewalt: Arbeiten von Carlos Garaicoa, Meira Marreo und José Toirac, Sandra Ramos, Adrián Fernández, Adriamna Continua, Frank Mujica Chávez, Mabel Poblet Pujol, Osvaldo González Aguiar, Humberto Díaz oder Frank Martínez, um nur einige wenige zu nennen.

II

Was bedeutet es für eine junge deutsche Künstlerin, nach Havanna zu gehen, gerade jetzt, um die Protagonisten der Kunst des Boxens und ihr Umfeld festzuhalten? Sich einer Subkultur zu nähern, die in radikaler Differenz steht zu ihrem eigenen soziokulturellen Kontext? Mit der Kamera in die Fremde zu ziehen und die andere Kultur in Bilder zu bannen, hat eine lange Geschichte und Generationen von Vorbildern. Und obgleich alles erkundet zu sein scheint und die frühere Mühsal und Gefahr der Reise sich weitgehend erledigt haben, bleiben die Anforderungen an den Fotografen doch die gleichen: Empathie, Zuneigung, Neugierde, die Fähigkeit einzutauchen, ein stückweit zumindest, um die neue Welt zu verstehen und das Vertrauen der Menschen zu gewinnen, mit denen er arbeiten will, darüber hinaus Recherche, Hartnäckigkeit,

Portrait and Milieu. El Boxeo in La Habana
The Photographs of Katharina Alt

Petra Giloy-Hirtz

I

"Un nuevo dia," the official organ of the Comité Central del Partido Comunista de Cuba quoted the words US President Barack Obama spoke during his "historic visit" at a press conference in the **teatro** of the Palacio de la Revolución on March 21, 2016. Four days later, speaking in Spanish, Mick Jagger addressed the 500,000 cheering people who had flocked to the Rolling Stones concert at the Ciudad Deportiva in Havana: "We know that for many years it has been difficult to hear our music in Cuba, but we are playing here. I also think that the times are finally changing." Springtime in Cuba: Raúl Castro extends his hand, no matter how much his elderly brother, Fidel, keeps invoking the goals of the revolution of 1959. What a moment!

Still, Cuba will for a long time continue to be a backdrop for the pictures for which it is famous and loved. Palaces and mansions, marvelous architecture, ranging from historicist to boldly modern, now often dilapidated structures with peeling

paint, relics of a once proudly resplendent time; and the old cars with their great colors, **mágico, místico**, endlessly photographed and compiled in lavish coffee-table books—a seductive yet limited visual vocabulary relying on nostalgia, melancholy, and the fascination of decadence. The image of the country in contemporary Cuban photography looks different; think, for instance, of the work of Alberto Korda from the 1950s and 1960s or that of José A. Figueroa. Photographers of the post-revolutionary era from 1990 to the present frequently offer socially and culturally critical commentary on such Cuban stereotypes.[1]

Cuban visual arts—painting, drawing, sculpture, installation, or video—are likewise devoid of that romanticism of the exotic gaze. They reflect on the historical, political, social, and cultural context of Cuba, on revolution, fleeing, emigration, censorship, and violence—the works of Carlos Garaicoa, Meira Marreo, and José Toirac, Sandra Ramos, Adrián Fernández, Adriamna Continua, Frank Mujica Chávez, Mabel Poblet

Pujol, Osvaldo González Aguiar, Humberto Díaz, and Frank Martínez, to mention only a few.

II

What does it mean for a young woman artist from Germany to go to Havana in this day and age, and try to capture the protagonists of the art of boxing and their milieu, try to approach a subculture that is radically different from her own socio-cultural context? There is a long history of generations of role models going abroad with their cameras and recording another culture in pictures. And although it seems that everything has already been explored and the erstwhile hardship and danger of traveling have by and large been taken care of, the demands on the photographer remain the same; empathy, devotion, curiosity, the ability to immerse oneself, at least to a certain degree, in order to understand the new world and gain the trust of the people with whom one wants to work, and, on top of this, research, doggedness, patience—and a good eye. Katharina Alt has all of

Geduld – und das gute Auge. Katharina Alt hat all das. Die soziale und sinnliche Logik dieses Sports erschließt sie sich über den »fremden Blick«, über eine »unmittelbare Fotografie«. Sie ist beobachtend, Zaungast und nicht Mitglied, wie Loïc Wacquant es für seine Sozialstudien über den Körper des Boxers und die Macht der Gesellschaft im schwarzen Ghetto der South Side von Chicago zu sein versuchte, indem er sich für mehrere Jahre der Szene eines lokalen Boxclubs anschloss und die strenge Disziplin der Boxer, das Training wie auch das gesamte Leben außerhalb des Gyms übernahm.[2]

Es ist faszinierend zu beobachten, wie Katharina Alt mit ihren Protagonisten umgeht, wie sie den Mann platziert, ohne viel künstliches Arrangement, aber dezidiert, etwa auf dem Platz vor El Trejo, der berühmten Boxschule in La Habana Vieja, den ein eingestürztes Haus freigegeben hat, oder vor der Fassade der Kirche in der Nachbarschaft. Wie sie mit ihm spricht, ihn ermutigt, ihn bittet, das T-Shirt abzulegen, **relajado** – denn sich gelöst zu stellen, sich der Kamera preiszugeben, ist auch für einen Boxer, der ja nicht als Star posiert oder in seinem Element auf der Bühne, sondern sich als Mensch zeigt, nicht per se einfach. Nur durch den Prozess

des Vertrauens und der Verständigung gelingt es der Künstlerin, dass jene Idole und die Institutionen dieses Sports ihr großzügig Eingang gewähren in die Trainingsstätten wie in das private Zuhause. Nur so können diese einfühlsamen Bilder entstehen. Sie sind ästhetische Aufzeichnungen eines Milieus, das maßgeblicher Teil kubanischer Identität und Kultur ist. Sie erzählen von der Lebensform des Boxens, ihren Ritualen, Regeln, Gewohnheiten, vom Alltag des Trainings und dem Fest des Kampfes, von Gelassenheit und Leidenschaft.

III

Nicht nur für die großen Namen interessiert sich Katharina Alt, für die Legenden der Vergangenheit und der Gegenwart, wie Lázaro Álvarez, Joahnys Argilagos, Yasniel Toledo, Yosvany Veitía, Arlen López, Julio César La Cruz, Erislandy Savón, Felix Savon sowie Emilio Correa sr. und jr. Sie will die ganze Szene einfangen, auch die Kinder, die in den Hinterhöfen von Havanna ihre ersten Boxerfahrungen machen, und die wenigen Frauen, die übrigens von offiziellen Wettkämpfen ausgeschlossen sind, wie die junge Dayamaivis Ruiz Pérez, die sie in der Sala Kid Chocolate in Havanna trifft, aber auch die Coachs wie Jordenis Colas Preval, die Medizi-

ner und Schiedsrichter, Situationen von Training und Kampf. Die Menschen interessieren sie – die Schauplätze erzählt sie gleich mit. Figur und Umgebung, Individuum und gesellschaftlicher Kontext erscheinen in ihren Bildern als eine Einheit.

Im Gegensatz zu Studioaufnahmen entstehen diese Fotografien spontan, mit einfachen technischen Mitteln; nicht immer ist Zeit, die Szene zu arrangieren. Aber gerade in der Vitalität des Situativen, in der emotionalen Qualität und nicht in der technischen Brillanz liegt die Stärke dieser Bilder. Weil sie den Einzelnen zeigen und die Gemeinschaft, die Welt, in der er lebt, das Private und das Öffentliche, wohnt ihnen eine kraftvolle soziale Komponente inne. Im Festhalten der Lebensbedingungen, der häuslichen Sphäre, der Straßen und Plätze haben sie wie nebenbei einen politischen Impetus und werden so, gerade in Zeiten gesellschaftlichen Wandels, zum historischen Zeugnis. Die Bilder sind vielschichtig. Künstlerisches und soziales Engagement fallen in eins. Wo die einen die verehrte Ikone betrachten, lesen die anderen die soziale Kommentierung des Bildes. Wo diese fasziniert sind von der Schönheit der Körper oder der pittoresquen Straßenszene und den farbenfrohen Interieurs, richten jene ihr

that. The social and sensuous logic of the sport reveals itself to her through the "gaze of the other," through "immediate photography." She is observant, an onlooker and not an insider, as Loïc Wacquant tried to be for his social study on the body of the boxer and the power of society in the black ghetto of Chicago's South Side, by associating himself for several years with the local boxing club scene and by adopting the boxers' strict discipline, both in training and in life outside the gym.[2]

It is fascinating to observe how Katharina Alt deals with her protagonists, how she positions the man without much artificial arrangement, yet decidedly—for instance, in the space in front of El Trejo, the famous boxing academy in La Habana Vieja that came about when a house collapsed, or in front of the façade of the neighborhood church. How she talks to him, encourages him, asks him to take off his T-shirt, **relajado**—after all, posing in a relaxed manner, exposing oneself to the camera does not come easy to a boxer who, rather than posturing like a star or in his element on the stage, is presenting himself as a human being. It is only through a process of trust and understanding that the artist gets the idols and the institutions of this sport to generously

grant her access both to training venues and private homes. These sensitive photographs could not have been taken any other way. They are aesthetic records of a milieu that is an essential part of Cuban identity and culture. They tell of the lifestyle of boxing, its rituals, rules, customs, of the daily routine of training and the celebration of the boxing match, of composure and passion.

III

Katharina Alt is not just interested in the big names, the legends of the past and present such as Lázaro Álvarez, Joahnys Argilagos, Yasniel Toledo, Yosvany Veitía, Arlen López, Julio César La Cruz, Erislandy Savón, Felix Savon, and Emilio Correa Sr. and Jr. She wants to capture the entire scene, including the kids who make their first acquaintance with boxing in the backyards of Havana, and the few women who, incidentally, are barred from official matches, such as the young Dayamaivis Ruiz Pérez, whom she encounters at the Sala Kid Chocolate in Havana, as well as the coaches, such as Jordenis Colas Preval, the medics and referees, situations from training and matches. She is interested in the people—the settings just become part of her stories. Figure and surroundings, the individual and his

or her social context, appear as a single entity in her photographs.

Unlike studio photographs, these pictures are created spontaneously, with basic technical means; there is not always time to arrange the scene. Yet the strength of these pictures lies precisely in the vitality of the situational, in their emotional quality, rather than in their technical brilliance. In showing individuals and the community, the world in which they live, the private and the public, they have a powerful social component. As they capture the living conditions, the domestic sphere, the streets and squares, they have, almost incidentally, a political impetus which makes them historical evidence, especially in times of social change. The pictures are multilayered. Artistic dedication and social commitment converge. While some see the revered icon, others read the photograph's social commentary. While the former may be fascinated with the beauty of the bodies or the picturesque street scenes and colorful interiors, the latter focus on the social background of the protagonists who are, invariably, Cubans with African roots—a masculine world which the artist encounters with sympathy. Her aim is to create a humane, dignified picture. She portrays each person individually and

Augenmerk auf die soziale Herkunft der Protagonisten, ausschließlich Kubaner mit afrikanischen Wurzeln. Eine maskuline Welt. Die Künstlerin begegnet ihr mit Sympathie, sie will ein humanes, würdevolles Bild. Jeden Einzelnen porträtiert sie individuell und gibt der Arbeit als Titel seinen Namen.

Poetische Stillleben ergänzen die Porträts. Ein Gespür für Komposition, Farben und Strukturen zeichnet sie aus, die Aufmerksamkeit für Details, die wie zufällig aufgelesen am Rande erscheinen: »Accessoires« wie Handschuhe, Helme und Bandagen, eine Waage, ein hingeworfenes Handtuch, der verlassene Ring. Atmosphärische Bilder der Ruhe im Spiel von Licht und Schatten, im Morgengrauen oder in der Abenddämmerung, unter freiem Himmel und im geschlossenen Raum.

Im Vorraum des Centro Sportivo Rafael Trejo sind mit Papierblumen geschmückte Fotos an die Wand geheftet: »Nuestros Campeones« – Fidel Castro und Nelson Mandela beglückwünschen hier einen Sieger. Und gleich daneben ist die »Mission« der Dirección Municipal de Deportes angeschlagen: »Utilizar un sistema de superación dirigido a la constante formación de los recursos humanos preparados con profesionalidad para cumplir con los objectivos de la entidad y programas de la revolución.«[3] Die kubanischen Boxer, bis vor Kurzem noch Amateure – bevor Fidel Castros Verbot des Profiboxens aufgehoben wurde –, gelten als stilistisch elegant, äußerst behende und technisch perfekt. Ihre zahlreichen Siege haben ihnen in aller Welt großen Respekt eingebracht. Erfolg gewährt ihnen durch ein System der Auszeichnungen und Belohnungen Privilegien und ein besseres Leben in einer Gesellschaft des Mangels. Aber nicht das leuchtet aus ihren Gesichtern, viel eher das Wissen um Zugehörigkeit, der Stolz, Teil dieser Kommunität zu sein, Willenskraft, Körperlichkeit, Energie. Es sind entspannte Antlitze, oft voller Anmut und alles andere als brutal oder »zugerichtet«: ernsthaft, ruhig, wache Augen, manche versonnen zugleich – der junge Boxer mit Helm und Handschuhen oder der olympische Champion Emilio Correa Bayeux jr. In einigen Bildern selbstbewusst ihren echt goldenen Schmuck tragend, Ringe, Ketten, Uhren, oft Trophäen ihres Sieges: Jene Athleten, exemplarische Typen des sportlichen Wettstreits, von großer Könnerschaft und außerordentlichen Kräften und darin Leitbilder, haben noch immer etwas »von der Aura der Wundermänner archaischer Zeiten« um sich.[4]

IV

Ein kurzer Blick auf die kubanische zeitgenössische Kunst zeigt die Omnipräsenz des Themas Boxen. Douglas Pérez zum Beispiel, der sich in seiner Malerei nach eigenen Worten mit der »popular culture of the Afro-Cubans« auseinandersetzt, verbindet das Motiv des Boxens mit Materialien wie Fäden, Muscheln und Gewebe sowie Techniken afrikanischer Handarbeit.

Für seine Serie **Requiem,** einer Chronik Kubas des 20. Jahrhunderts, die auf der fototechnischen Bearbeitung von Briefmarken beruht, wählt Adrián Fernández auch das Motiv der Boxkämpfer aus (**Untitled #6**).

Die elfte Ausgabe der **Bienal de La Habana** im Jahr 2012 präsentierte Boxperformances (**The Fight, The Gloves**) von Humberto Vélez. »[…] als lateinamerikanischer Künstler halte ich es für wichtig«, sagt er, »die andere Art von künstlerischer Sprache zu gestalten oder sichtbar zu machen, die wir heute haben und die nicht nur von der abendländischen Tradition herkommt, sondern vornehmlich von anderen Kontinenten […].«[5]

Boxen als Element der populären Kultur ist offenkundig ein reizvolles Thema auch im internationalen Kunstkontext, weil es – transloziert vom sportlichen in einen ästhetischen Zusammenhang, ohne Kunst im her-

uses the names of the sitters as titles of the works.

Poetic still lifes complement the portraits. These works are characterized by an intuitive sense of composition, color, and structure, by an attention to details which appear marginal, as if randomly picked up: "accessories" such as gloves, head guards, scales, a towel that seems to have been carelessly thrown to the ground, the deserted ring. Atmospheric images of tranquility in the play of light and shadow, at dawn or dusk, outdoors and in closed spaces.

In the lobby of the Centro Sportivo Rafael Trejo photographs decorated with paper flowers are pinned to the wall: "Nuestros Campeones." We see Fidel Castro and Nelson Mandela congratulating a winner. Posted right next to it is the mission statement of the Dirección Municipal de Deportes: "Utilizar un sistema de superación dirigido a la constante formación de los recursos humanos preparados con professionalidad para cumplir con los objectivos de la entidad y programas de la revolución."[3] The Cuban boxers who, until the recent lifting of Fidel Castro's ban on professional boxing, were still amateurs, are considered stylistically elegant, extremely nimble, and technically perfect. Their countless victories have earned them great respect throughout the world. Through a system of awards and rewards success translates into privileges and a better life for them in a society of scarcity. But this is not what makes their faces shine; rather, it is their sense of belonging, their pride in being part of this community, willpower, physicality, energy. Their faces are relaxed, often graceful, and anything but brutal or battered; the eyes serious, calm, alert, and in some cases at the same time pensive—the young boxer with head guards and gloves or the Olympic champion Emilio Correa Bayeux Jr., who some pictures show self-confidently wearing their real gold jewelry, rings, necklaces, watches, often trophies of their victories. Exemplary characters in sporting competition with great skills and extraordinary strengths and, as such, role models, these athletes still have some of "the aura of […] the miracle men of archaic times" about them.[4]

IV

A cursory look at contemporary Cuban art reveals the omnipresence of the subject of boxing. Douglas Pérez, for instance, who, in his own words, explores the "popular culture of the Afro-Cubans" in his paintings, combines the subject of boxing with materials such as threads, shells, and fabrics as well as with techniques of African handicraft.

For his **Requiem** series, a chronicle of 20th-century Cuba based on the photographic manipulation of postage stamps, Adrián Fernández likewise picks the subject of boxers (**Untitled #6**).

The 11th **Bienal de La Habana** in 2012 featured boxing performances (**The Fight, The Gloves**) by Humberto Vélez. Vélez explains: "[…] as a Latin American artist I think it is important just to create or show the different kind of language that we have in art now and that not only comes from the Western tradition, but especially from other continents […]."[5]

Boxing as an element of popular culture is obviously an appealing subject in the international art context as well, because when it is removed from the world of sports to an aesthetic context without being art in the traditional sense, it takes on a new connotation and provides access to new meanings and experiences. As early as 2007, Tate Modern in London showed Humberto Vélez's boxing performance **The Fight**, which in **Ethnographic Terminalia**, a 2011 exhibition on the crossovers between art and anthropology in Montreal, was complemented by dance and music. As part of the opening event of the **Festival of Independents** at the Haus der Kunst in Munich on

kömmlichen Sinne zu sein, eine neue Konnotation erhält und einen Zugang zu neuen Bedeutungen und Erfahrungen eröffnet. Die Tate Modern in London zeigte schon 2007 Humberto Vélez' Boxperformance **The Fight** und die Ausstellung zum Crossover von Kunst und Anthropologie in Montreal 2011, **Ethnographic Terminalia**, ergänzte sie durch Tanz und Musik. Im Rahmen der Eröffnungsveranstaltung des von Anna Schneider kuratierten **Festival of Independents** im Haus der Kunst unter der Leitung von Okwui Enwezor in München am 15. November 2013 fand eine spektakuläre Boxveranstaltung statt, der Hunderte von Menschen gebannt folgten. **Full Service – Savages against Whites** (2012–2014), ein Video mit einem spontanen Boxkampf zwischen einem weißen Amerikaner und einem Paiute, zeigte Cyrill Lachauer in seiner Einzelausstellung in der Villa Stuck in München 2015 – die Reihe ließe sich verlängern.

V

Mit dem Buch **Boxing Cuba** legt Katharina Alt ihre erste Monografie vor. Was hat sie bisher gemacht? Was interessiert sie? Wie ist ihr Selbstverständnis als Künstlerin? Den Schwerpunkt ihrer Arbeit hat sie früh festgelegt. Es ist ihr Interesse an bestimmten gesellschaftlichen Gruppen, das sie treibt, und so schloss sie mit dem eindrucksvollen Zyklus **Roma 20 mm** über eine Roma-Siedlung in der Ostslowakei ihr Studium an der Fachhochschule in München als Jahrgangsbeste ab. Es folgten Auftragsarbeiten für zahlreiche Magazine und Tageszeitungen: Porträts und soziokulturelle Studien. Als freie Künstlerin entwickelte Katharina Alt ihren eigenen Stil. Für ein halbes Jahr unterhielt sie ein kleines Studio in Indien und lud Menschen dorthin ein. Es entstanden klassische Porträts in Schwarz-Weiß – das ist ihr liebstes Sujet – konzeptuell die immer gleiche Situation und Pose: der Protagonist vor schwarzer Wand, die Hände offen und im zweiten Bild die Sohlen der Füße, weil jene Oberflächen viel aussagen über das Leben und Wesen des Porträtierten. Ein Faible für ältere Menschen hat Katharina Alt, vielleicht, so erklärt sie sich das, weil ihre Mutter früh gestorben und sie bei den Großeltern aufgewachsen ist. Und so arbeitet sie an einer erstaunlichen Werkreihe von Porträts von Hundertjährigen und noch Älteren, die bald als Publikation erscheinen soll.

Eine repräsentative Auswahl ihrer neuen Fotografien unter dem Titel **Boxing Cuba** (in den Formaten von 52 cm × 74 cm und 124 cm × 84 cm, auf Innova Fiber Print Paper, in klassischem Rahmen, ohne Passepartout) eröffnet im Frühjahr 2016 im Museum Fünf Kontinente in München, das sich primär Kunstwerken nichteuropäischer Herkunft widmet. Die Ausstellung wird vermutlich über die Kunstszene hinaus ein an anderen Kulturen interessiertes Publikum anziehen und zudem eines, das aus der Welt des Boxens kommt – und jeder wird sicher einen anderen Blick auf diese Bilder haben. Teil der Ausstellung, die unter der Schirmherrschaft des Auswärtigen Amts der Bundesrepublik Deutschland steht, ist ein Boxring, ortsspezifische künstlerische Installation und reale Schaubühne des Kampfes zugleich. Repräsentativ für alle wird einer der Helden anwesend sein, Hector Vinent Charón, vom Museum eingeladen als **curator in residence**. Für Kuba entsteht ein spezielles Portfolio von Katharina Alts Fotografien. So wird gleich einem Gabentausch etwas vom Reichtum, den diese Bilder hierher transferiert haben, zurückgegeben.

November 15, 2013, curated by Anna Schneider and attended by its director Okwui Enwezor, a spectacular boxing event took place that mesmerized hundreds of people. **Full Service— Savages against Whites** (2012–14), a video of an ad hoc boxing match between a white American and a Paiute, was shown by Cyrill Lachauer in his 2015 solo exhibition at the Villa Stuck in Munich. And the list could go on.

V

Boxing Cuba is the first monograph Katharina Alt has produced. What has she been doing to date? What interests her? How does she see herself as an artist? She defined the focus of her work early on. What drives her is an interest in specific social groups. Accordingly, her final project at the Munich University of Applied Sciences, where she graduated as the best in her class, was an impressive series about a Romani settlement in East Slovakia titled **Roma 20 mm**. This was followed by commissions for numerous magazines and newspapers: portraits and socio-cultural studies. As an independent artist, Katharina Alt developed her own style. For six months she maintained a small studio in India and invited people to come and visit. This resulted in classical portraits in black and white—her favorite subject—that feature conceptually the same situation and pose throughout: the protagonists in front of a black wall, showing the palms of their hands and, in the second image, the soles of their feet, because those surfaces say a lot about the lives and characters of the sitters. Katharina Alt has a predilection for older people, perhaps—as she explains it to herself—because her mother died at an early age and she grew up with her grandparents. And so she is working on an astonishing series of portraits of centenarians and even older people that is soon to be published as a photobook.

In the spring of 2016 a representative selection of her new photographs titled **Boxing Cuba** (dimensions 52 cm × 74 cm [20 in × 29 in] and 124 cm × 84 cm [49 in × 33 in], printed on Innova Fiber Print Paper and mounted in a classic frame without mat) will go on view at the Five Continents Museum in Munich, an institution primarily devoted to non-European art. Beyond the art crowd this exhibition is likely to draw people interested in other cultures as well as visitors from the world of boxing—with each of them bound to have another perspective on the works. The exhibition, which is under the patronage of The German Federal Foreign Office, includes a boxing ring, both as a site-specific artistic installation and an actual stage for matches. To represent them all, one of the Cuban heroes will be present: Hector Vinent Charón has been invited by the museum to be curator-in-residence. A special portfolio of Katharina Alt's photographs is being compiled for Cuba. In this manner, as in an exchange of gifts, some of the richness transferred here by these photographs will be returned.

Erislandy Savón Cotilla, 91 kg
Goldmedaille bei der Weltmeisterschaft 2015 in Doha
Gold medal at the 2015 World Boxing Championships in Doha

Lázaro Jorge Álvarez Estrada, 60 kg
Goldmedaille bei den Weltmeisterschaften 2011 in Baku, 2013 in Almaty und
2015 in Doha, Bronzemedaille bei den Olympischen Spielen 2012 in London
Gold medal at the 2011 World Boxing Championships in Baku, 2013 in Almaty
and 2015 in Doha, bronze medal at the 2012 Olympic Games in London

Robeisy Ramírez, 56 kg
Goldmedaille bei den Olympischen Spielen 2012 in London
Gold medal at the 2012 Olympic Games in London

Emmanuel Reyes Pla, 81 kg

Armando Martínez, 60 kg

Luis Oliva Gener, 64 kg

Arlen Lopez Cardona, 75 kg
Goldmedaille bei der Weltmeisterschaft 2015 in Doha
Gold medal at the 2015 World Boxing Championships in Doha

Joahnys Oscar Argilagos Perez, 49 kg
Goldmedaille bei der Weltmeisterschaft 2015 in Doha
Gold medal at the 2015 World Boxing Championships in Doha

Yasnier Toledo López, 64 kg
Silbermedaille bei der Weltmeisterschaft 2015 in Doha, Bronzemedaille bei den Olympischen Spielen 2012 in London
Silver medal at the 2015 World Boxing Championships in Doha,
bronze medal at the 2012 Olympic Games in London

Julio César La Cruz, 81 kg
Goldmedaille bei den Weltmeisterschaften 2011 in Baku, 2013
in Almaty und 2015 in Doha
Gold medal at the 2011 World Boxing Championships in Baku,
2013 in Almaty and 2015 in Doha

Yosbani Veitía, 52 kg
Silbermedaille bei der Weltmeisterschaft 2015 in Doha
Silver medal at the World Boxing Championships 2015 in Doha

Roniel Iglesias Sotolongo, 69 kg

Goldmedaille bei den Weltmeisterschaften 2009 in Mailand, Bronzemedaille bei den Olympischen Spielen 2008 in Peking und Goldmedaille
bei den Olympischen Spielen 2012 in London

Gold medal at the 2009 World Boxing Championships in Milan, bronze
medal at the 2008 Olympic Games in Beijing and gold medal at the 2012
Olympic Games in London

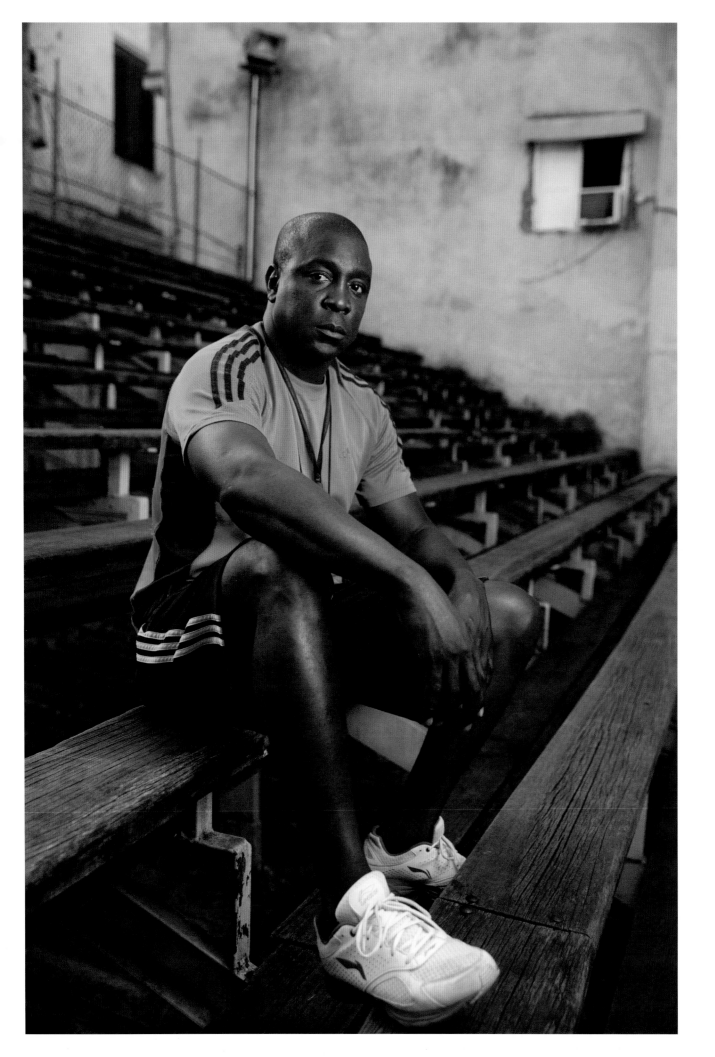

Héctor Vinent Charón
Sieger der Jugendweltmeisterschaften 1991 und 1992, Goldmedaille bei
den Weltmeisterschaften 1993 in Tampere und 1995 in Berlin, Goldmedaille
bei den Olympischen Spielen 1992 in Barcelona und 1996 in Atlanta
Winner of the Junior World Championships in 1991 and 1992, gold medal
at the 1993 World Boxing Championships in Tampere and 1995 in Berlin,
gold medal at the 1992 Olympic Games in Barcelona and 1996 in Atlanta

Emilio Correa Bayeux
Bronzemedaille bei der Weltmeisterschaft 2005 in Mianyang,
Silbermedaille bei den Olympischen Spielen 2008 in Peking
Bronze medal at the 2005 World Boxing Championships in
Mianyang, silver medal at the 2008 Olympic Games in Beijing

Emilio Correa Bayeux
Bronzemedaille bei der Weltmeisterschaft 2005 in Mianyang, Silbermedaille bei den Olympischen Spielen 2008 in Peking
Bronze medal at the 2005 World Boxing Championships in Mianyang,
silver medal at the 2008 Olympic Games in Beijing

Emilio Correa Vaillant
Goldemedaille bei den Olympischen Spielen 1972 in München
Gold medal at the 1972 Olympic Games in Munich

Dayamaivis Ruiz Pérez
Kid Chocolate Gym, Centro Habana

Pedro Orlando Reyes
In seinem Haus in Arrollo Naranjo, Habana
Goldmedaille bei der Weltmeisterschaft 1986 in Reno
und Silbermedaille bei der Weltmeisterschaft 1989 in Moskau
At his home in Arrollo Naranjo, Habana
Gold medal at the 1986 World Boxing Championships in Reno
and silver medal at the 1989 World Boxing Championships in Moscow

Félix Savón Fabre

In seinem Haus
Gewinner des Chemiepokals 1985, 1986, 1987 und 1996,
Goldmedaille bei den Weltmeisterschaften 1986 in Reno,
1989 in Moskau, 1991 in Sydney, 1993 in Tampere, 1995 in
Berlin, 1997 in Budapest und Silbermedaille bei der Welt-
meisterschaft 1999 in Houston, Goldmedaille bei den
Olympischen Spielen 1992 in Barcelona, 1996 in Atlanta
und 2000 in Sydney

At his home
Winner of the Chemiepokal 1985,1986,1987 and 1996, gold
medal at the 1986 World Boxing Championships in Reno,
1989 in Moscow, 1991 in Sydney, 1993 in Tampere, 1995
in Berlin, 1997 in Budapest and silver medal at the 1999
World Boxing Championships in Houston, gold medal at
the 1992 Olympic Games in Barcelona, 1996 in Atlanta and
2000 in Sydney

Yampier Hernández
Bronzemedaille bei den Olypmischen Spielen 2008 in Peking
Bronze medal at the 2008 Olympic Games in Beijing

Luis Felipe Martínez Sánchez
Silbermedaille bei der Weltmeisterschaft 1978 in Belgrad,
Bronzemedaille bei den Olympischen Spielen 1976 in Montreal
Silver medal at the 1978 World Boxing Championships in
Belgrade, bronze medal at the 1976 Olympic Games in Montreal

Jorge Alardo Castillo
Chef der Academia Provincial
Manager of the Academia Provincial

Sarbelio Fuentes Rodríguez
Ehemaliger Nationaltrainer
Former national team coach

Maikro Romero
Im Haus seiner Großeltern, Habana Vieja,
Goldmedaille bei der Weltmeisterschaft 1997 in Budapest,
Goldmedaille bei den Olympischen Spielen 1996 in Atlanta
At his grandparents' home, Habana Vieja,
Gold medal at the 1997 World Boxing Championships in
Budapest, gold medal at the 1996 Olympic Games in Atlanta

Ramón Duvalón
Silbermedaille bei den Olympischen Spielen
1976 in Montreal
Silver medal at the 1976 Olympic Games
in Montreal

Candelario Duvergel
Sieger der Panamerikanischen Spiele 1983 in Caracas und 1987
in Indianapolis, Bronzemedaille bei der Weltmeisterschaft 1991
in Sydney
Winner of the 1983 Pan American Games in Caracas and
1987 in Indianapolis, bronze medal at the 1991 World Boxing
Championships in Sydney

José Gómez Mustelier
Goldmedaille bei der Weltmeisterschaft 1978 in Belgrad,
Goldmedaille bei den Olympischen Spielen 1980 in Moskau
Gold medal at the 1978 World Boxing Championships
in Belgrade, gold medal at the 1980 Olympic Games in Moscow

Sixto Soria
Goldmedaille bei der Weltmeisterschaft 1978 in Belgrad,
Silbermedaille bei den Olympischen Spielen 1976 in Montreal
Gold medal at the 1978 World Boxing Championships in Belgrade,
silver medal at the 1976 Olympic Games in Montreal

Daniel Gubert Romero
Schiedsrichter, in seiner Wohnung
in San Miguel del Padrón, Habana
Referee, at his home in San Miguel
del Padrón, Habana

Jordenis Colas Preval
Trainer im Kid Chocolate Gym
Coach at Kid Chocolate Gym

Modesto Vazquez Basabe
Sportarzt
Sports doctor

Guillermo Santín de la Torre
Trainer im San Miguel del Padrón Gym
Coach at San Miguel del Padrón Gym

San Miguel del Padrón Gym, Habana

Junger Boxer im Roberto Balado Gym, La Lisa, Habana
Young boxer at Roberto Balado Gym, La Lisa, Habana

Junger Boxer im Roberto Balado Gym, La Lisa, Habana
Young boxer at Roberto Balado Gym, La Lisa, Habana

Junge und Vater, Rafael Trejo Gym, Habana Vieja
Boy and his father, Rafael Trejo Gym, Habana Vieja

Junge Boxer und ihre Trainer, Rafael Trejo Gym,
Habana Vieja (vorherige Doppelseite)
Young boxers and their coaches, Rafael Trejo Gym,
Habana Vieja (previous double page)

Nardo Mestre Flores
Trainer im Rafael Trejo Gym
Coach at Rafael Trejo Gym

World Series Boxing, Season VI, La Ciudad Deportiva, Habana
Cuba Domadores vs. Ukraine Otamans
Arlen Lopez Cardona

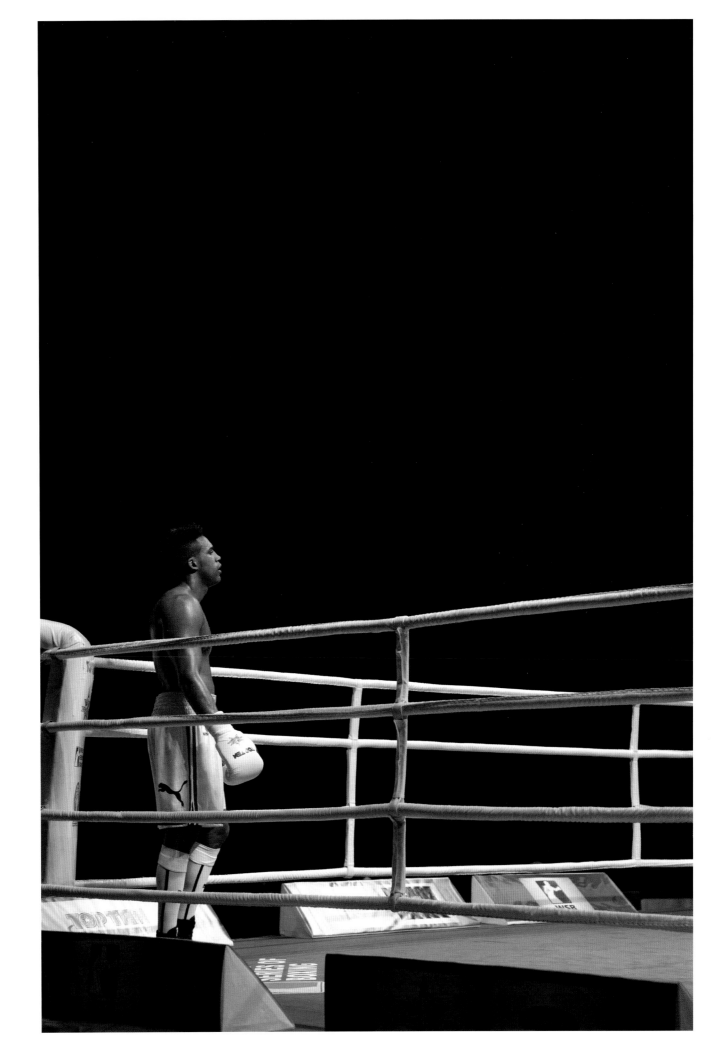

World Series Boxing, Season VI, La Ciudad Deportiva, Habana
Cuba Domadores vs. Ukraine Otamans
Ring girl

World Series Boxing, Season VI, La Ciudad Deportiva, Habana
Cuba Domadores vs. Ukraine Otamans
Zuschauer
Spectators

World Series Boxing, Season VI, La Ciudad Deportiva, Habana
Cuba Domadores vs. Ukraine Otamans
Robeisy Ramírez

2016 – das Jahr Kubas

Claudia Strand

Der »Giraldo Córdova Cardín« – Kubas Boxer im internationalen Vergleich

Die Luft steht heiß in der Sala Kid Chocolate. Hier in Havanna wird eines der landesweit wichtigsten Boxturniere ausgetragen, der »Torneo Internacional de Boxeo Giraldo Córdova Cardín«. Kubanische Boxtalente stellen sich in dieser Halle den großen nationalen und internationalen Gegnern. Das alles geschieht bei Höchsttemperaturen und zur unaufgeregten Stimme des Kommentators. Die Sala hallt wider von tanzenden Füßen und dumpfen Schlägen.

Arlen López ist so ein Talent. 1,78 Meter groß kämpft er im Mittelgewicht gegen Omar Capote. López tänzelt vor seinem Gegner, geht in Deckung und setzt Capote konstante Jabs (direkte Geraden). Dann nutzt er die Gelegenheit zum Powerpunch. López tritt für seine Provinz Guantanamo im Süden an, Capote für Granma im Südosten des Landes. Kubanische »Südstaatler« in angespannter Aufmerksamkeit. Sie kämpfen auf Augenhöhe.

Erst 23-jährig gehört López zu den Hoffnungen des kubanischen Boxsports und hat sich 2015 in der World Series of Boxing für die Olympischen Spiele 2016 qualifizieren können. Auch die Weltmeisterschaft 2015 in Doha hat López dank seiner präzisen Technik in den Armen und in der schnellen Beinarbeit gewonnen. Sieger ist er auch in diesem Kampf gegen Omar Capote.

Boxen – Kubas Exportschlager Nummer eins im Sport

Das Boxen ist ein erfolgreiches kubanisches Exportprodukt, fast wie Tabak, Zucker, Kaffee oder Rum. Adrenalin statt Alkohol, unterlegt mit der Leichtfüßigkeit des **Buena Vista Social Club**. Jenem zum Kult avancierten Musikalbum, das die Musiker Juan de Marcos González und Ry Cooder zusammenstellten – Cuba meets USA. Felix Savón schlägt Ray Mercer im Länderkampf Kuba-USA 1988. Die Sportevents balancieren auf dem schmalen Grat zwischen Leichtigkeit, Politik und archaischem Kämpferwillen. Boxen

in Kuba ist rhythmisches Feeling, definiert von Schweiß, gnadenloser Disziplin und harter Arbeit. Wer hier hoch hinaus will, muss klein anfangen.

Sala Kid Chocolate – Havannas feine Adresse im Boxsport

Die »Sala polivalente Kid Chocolate« liegt mitten in der Altstadt von Havanna. Genau dort, wo das Herz des Viertels La Habana Vieja schlägt und karibisches Lebensgefühl sozialistischer Prägung den Takt vorgibt. Ihr gegenüber steht ein Prunkbau aus blendend hellem Kalkstein, eine Art Replik des Washingtoner Kapitols, wie feine Ironie: Das Capitolio war früher Sitz des Repräsentantenhauses – ein großer herrschaftlicher Prunkbau. Die Sala Kid Chocolate scheint seine sportliche, wenn auch architektonisch eher bescheidene Entsprechung zu sein. Doch ist sie, wenn man so will, die feine Adresse des Boxsportes in Kuba. Denn hier kämpfen die Besten der Besten unter den Boxern beim Giraldo Córdova Cardín.

2016—The Year of Cuba
Claudia Strand

The "Giraldo Córdova Cardín"— Cuba's Boxers by International Standards

The air is hot and stagnant in the Sala Kid Chocolate. The "Torneo Internacional de Boxeo Giraldo Córdova Cardín," one of the country's most important boxing tournaments, is held here in Havana. Cuban boxing talents face the strongest national and international opponents in this hall. This all happens at extreme temperatures and is accompanied by the calm voice of the commentator. The Sala echoes with the sounds of nimbly dancing feet and thudding punches.

Arlen López is one of those local talents. Five feet ten inches tall, he is facing Omar Capote in a middleweight fight. López skips in front of his opponent, ducking and throwing constant jabs at Capote. Then, spotting his moment, he seizes the opportunity for a power punch. López is representing Guantanamo Province in the south and Capote Granma Province in the country's southeast: the Cuban southerners are tensely focused, as they fight as equals.

Only 23 years old, López is one of the great hopes of Cuban boxing, who in 2015 managed to qualify for the 2016 Olympic Games. Thanks to his precise punching technique and fast footwork, López also won the 2015 world championship in Doha. He wins this fight against Omar Capote, too.

Boxing—Cuba's Top Sporting Export

Boxing is one of Cuba's most successful Cuban export, much the same as tobacco, sugar, coffee, or rum. Adrenaline instead of alcohol, accompanied by the lightfootedness of **Buena Vista Social Club**, the album put together by musicians Juan de Marcos González and Ry Cooder that achieved cult status: Cuba meets the USA. Felix Savón beat Ray Mercer in the 1988 match Cuba vs. USA. Such sporting events walk the fine line between lightness, politics, and an archaic will to fight. Boxing in Cuba is a rhythmic feeling, defined by sweat, merciless discipline, and hard work. Anyone here who wants to get to the top must start at the bottom.

Sala Kid Chocolate—Havana's Best Address in Boxing

The "Sala polivalente Kid Chocolate" is located at the very heart of La Habana Vieja, where a socialistically informed Caribbean lifestyle sets the rhythm. Across from it is an impressive dazzlingly bright limestone building, a kind of replica of the Washington Capitol—a kind of gentle irony. The Capitolio used to be the seat of the House of Representatives—a large, grand, majestic building. The Sala Kid Chocolate seems to be a sporty, architecturally rather modest counterpart. Yet it is arguably the best address in boxing in Cuba, for this is where the top boxers fight in the Giraldo Córdova Cardín.

"El Boxeo Soy Yo"—Kid Chocolate, the Best Boxer of All Time

One of the boxing champions was the inspiration for the facility's name. The Sala Kid Chocolate is named after the first Cuban world champion in professional boxing, Eligio Sardiñas Montalvo, better known as Kid Chocolate. **El boxeo soy yo**—"I am boxing"—a

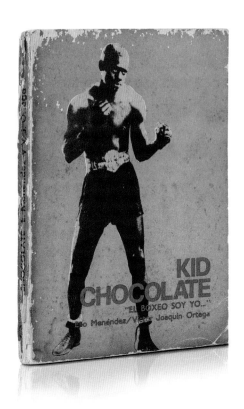

Elio Menéndez, Victor Joaquin Ortega, *Kid Chocolate.*
El boxeo soy yo …, Editorial ORBE, 1980

»El boxeo soy yo« – »Kid Chocolate«, der beste Boxer aller Zeiten

Einer der Boxchampions stand Pate für den Namen der Halle. Die Sala Kid Chocolate ist benannt nach dem ersten kubanischen Weltmeister im Profisport, Eligio Sardiñas Montalvo, bekannt als »Kid Chocolate«. »El boxeo soy yo« (»das Boxen bin ich«) – diese Aussage zeugt von nicht gerade geringem Selbstbewusstsein. Ein Athlet im Feder- und Superfedergewicht, schwergewichtig im Götterhimmel des Boxsportes. Derjenige, der das so locker von sich behauptete, wurde von der US-amerikanischen High Society in den Dreißigern bewundert und hofiert. Ein Lebemann im weißen Anzug auf dunkler Haut, von schönen Frauen umgeben. »Kid Chocolate« avancierte in dieser Rolle zum Urvater der kubanischen Amateurboxer und prägte mit seinem Kampfstil eine ganze Boxergeneration. Ein Konterboxer mit außergewöhnlicher Schlagkraft in der Rechten und guten Nehmerqualitäten. Elegant und tänzerisch mit dynamischer Beinarbeit gilt er heute als bester Boxer aller Zeiten.

Absolut leichtfüßig und unerreicht. In der International Boxing Hall of Fame, einer Art Hollywood Walk of Fame des Boxsports, war ihm der erste Stern sicher.

Karriere im Ausland – Trainerehren in Kuba

»Kid Chocolates« großspuriges Auftreten sollte einer ganzen Nation zu neuem Selbstbewusstsein verhelfen – zumindest beim Boxen. Kämpfen für eine bessere Zukunft. Das gilt auch heute. Er hatte es geschafft und verdiente im Profiboxen das große Geld, allerdings fern seiner Heimat. Als treuer Sohn Kubas kehrte er nach seiner Karriere Ende der Dreißiger zurück und arbeitete dort als Trainer. Bis zu seinem Tod lebte er von da an in bescheidenen Verhältnissen. Ganz im Dienste seiner Profession und seiner Landsleute, weshalb er noch immer verehrt wird wie ein Heiliger.

Große Namen im kubanischen Boxsport

Bilder von »Kid Chocolate« und manchem seiner Kollegen hängen im Eingang der Sala. Junge Talente treten hier gegen chinesische und venezolanische Boxer, Delegationen aus Brasilien und Kolumbien sowie nahezu die gesamte russische Equipe an. Klangvolle Namen zeugen von der großen Tradition des kubanischen Boxsportes. »Kid Gavilán«, Luis Rodríguez, Ultiminio »Sugar« Ramos, José »Mantequilla« Nápoles, Benny »Kid« Paret, »Niño« Valdés und natürlich Teófilo Stevenson, der noch heute als einer der ganz Großen gilt. Sie legten den Grundstein für eine erfolgsversprechende Zukunft. Denn Kuba ist heute ein Boxgigant. Allein bei den letzten Olympischen Spielen 2012 in London gab es zweimal Gold (Robeisy Ramírez im Fliegengewicht, Roniel Iglesias im Halbweltergewicht) und zwei Bronzemedaillen (Lázaro Álvarez im Bantamgewicht, Yasniel Toledo im Leichtgewicht) und damit mehr als für Russland oder die USA. Kuba investiert viel in den Sport und besonders in seine Boxer. Mit diesem Engagement holt man auch die Kids von der Straße und bringt sie rein in die Boxzentren, die sich über die ganze

Kid Gavilán

statement reflecting no small amount of self-esteem. An athlete competing at featherweight and super featherweight, yet a heavyweight in the pantheon of boxing. The one who had no qualms saying this of himself was admired and courted by American high society in the 1930s: a **bon vivant** in a white suit against dark skin, surrounded by beautiful women. In this role Kid Chocolate developed into the primal father of Cuban amateur boxers, and shaped an entire generation of boxers with his fighting style. A counter-puncher with extraordinary punching power in his right arm and extremely able to take punches. Elegant and dancer-like with dynamic footwork, he is today considered to be the best boxer of all time—perfectly light-footed and unrivaled. In the International Boxing Hall of Fame, a kind of Hollywood Walk of Fame of boxing, the first star was reserved for him.

Career Abroad—Honored as a Trainer in Cuba

Kid Chocolate's cocky bearing would help instill a new self-esteem in an entire nation—at least in boxing. Fighting for a better future. This is still true today. He had made it and made big money in professional boxing, albeit far from home. As a loyal son of Cuba he returned in the late 1930s, after his career had ended, and worked here as a trainer. From then on until his death he lived in modest circumstances, entirely devoted to his profession and his fellow countrymen, which is why he is still revered like a saint.

Big Names in Cuban Boxing

Pictures of Kid Chocolate and some of his fellow boxers hang in the entrance to the Sala. Here young talents take on Chinese and Venezuelan boxers, delegations from Brazil and Columbia

Insel verteilen. Hier darf sich jeder seine Zukunft erträumen, doch nur die Besten schaffen es, sie mit den Fäusten zu realisieren. Aus den Kleinen werden hier ganz Große.

Teófilo Stevenson – Kubas höchstdekorierter Boxchampion

Teófilo Stevenson, einer der großen Kämpfer des Landes, gewann den Giraldo Córdova Cardín 1971, 1972, 1974 bis 1979 und 1982. Elfmal kubanischer Meister, dreimal Weltmeister und zudem Olympiasieger, das ist schwergewichtige Superlative. Mit knappen 2 Metern und einer erbarmungslosen Rechten holte dieser Berg von einem Mann bereits mit zwanzig Jahren Gold in München. Dabei blieb er trotz lukrativer Millionengebote seiner Heimat treu und verweigerte sich hartnäckig dem Ausland. Die Ideale des Sozialismus schienen Fidel Castro mit dem profitablen Geschäft des Boxens jenseits der Insel nicht vereinbar zu sein, weshalb dieser 1964 kurzerhand den Profisport verbot. Mit markigen Sprüchen kommentierte Stevenson damals die zahlreichen Angebote aus den USA und der Welt: »Die Zuneigung von acht Millionen Kubanern ist mir wichtiger«, war sein respektables Statement. Millionen hätte man ihm für den Showdown mit Muhammad Ali bezahlt. Doch weit gefehlt. Wichtiger als Reichtum und Publicity, die seine Kollegen und allen voran sein berühmter Vorgänger »Kid Chocolate« im Ausland genossen, waren ihm Familie und Heimat. Stevenson blieb auch nach seiner aktiven Karriere dem Boxsport verbunden und arbeitete als Trainer im Nachwuchsbereich, treu seinem Motto, Zuhause ist da, wo mir die Herzen entgegenschlagen.

Havanna – Socialismo Tropical

Das Herz der Karibikinsel schlägt im Hafen von Havanna. Von hier aus gleitet der Blick weit übers Meer. Ernest Hemingways **Der alte Mann und das Meer** schildert den Kampf mit den Urgewalten der Natur und des Lebens

Manolo Cabalé Ruiz, *Teófilo Stevenson. Grande entre los grandes*, Editorial Científico-Técnica, 1985

as well as nearly the entire Russian team. Illustrious names are testament to the great tradition of Cuban boxing. Kid Gavilán, Luis Rodríguez, Ultiminio "Sugar" Ramos, José "Mantequilla" Nápoles, Benny "Kid" Paret, "Niño" Valdés and, of course, Teófilo Stevenson, who is still to this day considered one of the greatest. They laid the foundation for a promising future, for nowadays Cuba is a giant in world boxing. At the last Olympic Games in London in 2012 alone Cuba came away with two gold medals (Robeisy Ramírez in flyweight and Roniel Iglesias in light welterweight) and two bronze medals (Lázaro Álvarez in bantamweight and Yasniel Toledo in lightweight)—more than Russia or the USA. Cuba invests a lot in the sport and especially in its boxers. With this kind of commitment you also get the kids off the street and into the boxing centers that are scattered throughout the island. There everyone can dream about their future, but only the best will be able to make it a reality with their fists. Little ones turn into really big ones here.

Teófilo Stevenson—Cuba's Winningest Boxing Champion

Teófilo Stevenson, one of the country's great boxers, won the Giraldo Córdova Cardín in 1971, 1972, 1974–79, and 1982. Eleven-time Cuba champion,

three-time world champion as well as Olympic champion—these are heavyweight superlatives. At a height of six feet five inches and with a relentless right, this mountain of a man won gold when just a 20-year-old in Munich. Yet despite lucrative multi-million offers, he remained loyal to his home country and stuck tenaciously to his refusal to go abroad. Fidel Castro felt that the ideals of socialism were not compatible with the profitable business of boxing outside of the island, which is why he summarily banned professional sports in 1964. At the time Stevenson responded to the numerous offers from America and the world with pithy comments: "I prefer the affection of eight million Cubans," was his respectable response. He would have been paid millions for a showdown with Muhammad Ali. But no, far from it: family and home were more important to him than the wealth and publicity that his fellow boxers—with his famous predecessor, Kid Chocolate, leading the way—were enjoying abroad. Even after the end of his active career, Stevenson remained involved in boxing and worked as a trainer with young talents—true to his principle that home is where the hearts go out to me.

Havana—Socialismo Tropical

The heart of the Caribbean island beats in the harbor of Havana. From

here you can gaze far out across the sea. In **The Old Man and the Sea** Ernest Hemingway describes the battle with the elemental forces of nature and of life per se. It is similar in boxing: all alone, two men face one another in a fight using their fists, instinct, and a sense of timing. So, of course in Cuba, his adopted home country, Hemingway had to have the old man fight the battle with nature and wanted to learn to box himself—perhaps without as much success as in his writing, let alone what today's heroes at the Olympic Games are capable of.

Appropriately, just a couple of blocks away, you can try the legendary mojito or a daiquiri "Papa Doble"—the traditional Hemingway way without sugar but with twice the rum. In places such as these Cuba unfolds its own beauty and power expressed in a very special way through boxing. Someone else who realized this was Fidel Castro who preferred to have his men fight at home rather than elsewhere. He wanted to keep them in the country as far as possible, which was not always easy. Special talents look for challenges and, if necessary, will look abroad as well.

Fidel Castro's Politics of Limited Possibilities

Fidel Castro's ban made it impossible for an entire generation of boxers to

schlechthin. Beim Boxen ist das ähnlich. Ganz auf sich gestellt, mit Einsatz der Fäuste, Instinkt und dem Gefühl für den richtigen Augenblick stellen sich Mann gegen Mann im Zweikampf. Klar, dass Hemingway in seiner Wahlheimat Kuba ebenjenen alten Mann den Fight mit der Natur hat austragen lassen und auch das Boxen erlernen wollte. Mit vielleicht nicht ganz so großem Erfolg wie beim Schreiben, oder gar so, wie die heutigen Helden bei den Olympischen Spielen es vermögen.

Ein paar Ecken weiter gibt es dafür den legendären Mojito oder einen Daiquiri »Papa Doble« – ganz nach Hemingway-Manier ohne Zucker, aber mit doppeltem Rum. Kuba entfaltet an diesen Orten seine eigene Schönheit und Kraft, die im Boxsport ihren ganz besonderen Ausdruck findet. Das war auch Fidel Castro klar, der seine Männer lieber zu Hause kämpfen sah als anderswo. Er wollte sie möglichst im Land behalten, was nicht immer leicht war. Besondere Talente suchen eben die Herausforderung, und wenn es sein muss, auch im Ausland.

Fidel Castros Politik der begrenzten Möglichkeiten

Einer ganzen Boxgeneration machte es Fidel Castros Verbot völlig unmöglich, sich außerhalb des Amateurbereichs zu beweisen. Diesem Diktat wollten sich nicht alle beugen. Denn die Sportler verdienten auf der Insel nur einen Bruchteil dessen, was ihre Kollegen und berühmten Konkurrenten im Profibereich im Ausland erzielten. Dabei kommen die weltweit besten Boxer aus Kuba und dominieren das Amateurboxen ganz deutlich in allen Gewichtsklassen. Nicht wenige haben sich deshalb bei Kämpfen im Ausland abgesetzt. Hohe Verdienstmöglichkeiten, aber auch die Chancen, sich im sportlichen Wettkampf neuen Herausforderungen stellen zu dürfen, wollte sich so mancher nicht entgehen lassen.

Der »preußische Kubaner« – Yoan Pablo Hernández steigt aus dem Amateurgeschäft aus

Yoan Pablo Hernández ist einer von denen, die Kuba den Rücken kehrten, um als Profi Karriere zu machen. Als er seine Heimat verließ, war dies eine spontane Entscheidung, die er bis heute nicht bedauert. 2005 beim Chemiepokal in Halle nutzte er die Chance, in Deutschland zu bleiben, auch wenn sein Herz nach wie vor für die Karibikinsel schlägt.

Der Chemiepokal gilt als internationales Boxturnier von höchstem Rang. Es findet seit 1970 jährlich in Halle-Neustadt statt. Die Amateurboxer sollen auf dieser Plattform besser auf Großveranstaltungen wie die Olympischen Spiele vorbereitet werden. Für Kubas Athleten die Möglichkeit, sich mit internationalen Größen weitab von zu Hause zu messen. Gleichfalls aber auch eine Gelegenheit, ihre Heimat hinter sich zu lassen.

Damals erst 20-jährig war Hernández bereits Junioren-Weltmeister, Zweiter bei den Panamerikanischen Spielen und hatte an den Olympischen Spielen teilgenommen. Er wollte sich dem Profisport öffnen und im Training neue Wege beschreiten. Wenn es denn sein musste, eben auch fern der Heimat. Der »preußische Kubaner« mit deutschen Tugenden, wie sein Trainer immer wieder gerne betont, punktet mit Pünktlichkeit, Disziplin und Kämpferwillen. Für den Sauerland-Stall unter Ulli Wegner konnte das Ausnahmetalent zahlreiche Siege nach Hause bringen. Doch zunehmend machten ihm Verletzungen zu schaffen, und im September 2015 beendete der mittlerweile 31-Jährige seine Karriere.

Die Sportler verlassen ihr Land

Es trat ein, was das Verbot Castros eigentlich hatte verhindern sollen: Die besten Sportler wanderten ab. 2008, kurz vor den Olympischen Spielen in Peking, wurde das besonders schmerzhaft deutlich: Fünf der besten Boxer setzten sich ab. Zum ersten Mal kam das kubanische Nationalkader ohne

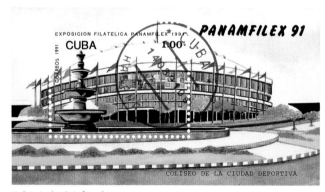

Kubanische Briefmarken
Cuban stamps

prove themselves beyond the amateur world. Not everyone was willing to bow to this dictate. After all, the athletes on the island earned just a fraction of what their fellow boxers and famous competitors made as professionals abroad. And yet the best boxers in the world come from Cuba, and clearly dominate amateur boxing in all weight divisions, so quite a few defected while they were fighting abroad. Many didn't want to miss out on the chance of making a lot of money and facing new challenges in competitive sport.

The "Prussian Cuban"—Yoan Pablo Hernández Leaves the Amateur Business

Yoan Pablo Hernández is one of those who turned his back on Cuba for a career as a pro. Leaving his home country was a spontaneous decision that, to this day, he has never regretted. During the 2005 Chemiepokal boxing tournament in Halle, Germany, he took the opportunity and stayed in Germany, even if his heart still belongs to the Caribbean island.

The Chemiepokal is considered one of the top international boxing tournaments. Held annually in Halle-Neustadt since 1970, it is intended as a platform for amateur boxers to better prepare for major events such as the Olympic Games. For Cuba's athletes it is a chance to compete with international greats far from home—yet also an opportunity to leave their home country behind.

Just 20 years old at the time, Hernández was already junior world champion and silver medalist at the Pan-American Games and he had competed in the Olympic Games. He wanted to be able to turn pro and explore new approaches in training— far from home if need be. The "Prussian Cuban" with German virtues, as his trainer likes to point out time and again, scores points for promptness, discipline, and fighting spirit. This exceptional talent was able to bring home numerous wins for the Sauerland team under Ulli Wegner. But Hernández suffered increasingly from injuries and in September 2015, by then 31 years old, he ended his career.

The Athletes Leave their Country

What Castro's ban was supposed to have prevented happened: the best athletes left the country. In 2008, just before the Olympic Games in Beijing, this became clear in a particularly painful way: five of the best boxers defected. For the first time, the Cuban national squad came home without a gold medal—a bitter disappointment for an island that is used to raking in medals. With a total of 34 Olympic medals the superpower of boxing is far ahead of all other countries with the exception of the USA. Today, Guillermo Rigondeaux is one of the most successful expatriate boxers as double world champion (WBA and WBO in super bantamweight). He lives far from home in Los Angeles where he trains at the Wild Card Boxing Club.

Boxing Reforms and a Gradual Opening-up

Raúl Castro's boxing reforms five years later have taken account of the exodus of boxing talents by means of some initial changes that are quite revolutionary. Assuming power gradually, Fidel's younger brother was also able to introduce reforms in Cuba, and in 2013 the time had come for sports. According to a decision of the Council of Ministers, athletes were allowed to sign professional contracts abroad starting in January 2014. Alberto Puig de la Barca, President of the Cuban Boxing Federation, signed an agreement whereby Cuba's amateur boxers joined the World Series of Boxing (WSB). The World Series consists of twelve teams with boxers from more than 50 countries competing in five different weight divisions. Eighty percent of the prize money will go to the athletes.

How this will affect the boxing style and the training methods at

Oldtimer in Havanna
Oldtimers in Havana

Goldmedaille nach Hause. Für die preisverwöhnte Insel eine herbe Enttäuschung. Denn der Boxgigant liegt mit 34 olympischen Medaillen weit vor allen anderen Nationen, ausgenommen den USA. Guillermo Rigondeaux ist heute als Doppelweltmeister (WBA und WBO im Superbantamgewicht) einer der erfolgreichsten Boxemigranten. Er lebt fern der Heimat in Los Angeles, wo er im Wild Card Boxing Club trainiert.

Boxreformen und eine schrittweise Öffnung

Raúl Castros Boxreformen haben der Abwanderung von Boxtalenten fünf Jahre später mit geradezu revolutionären ersten Veränderungen Rechnung getragen. Fidels jüngerer Bruder konnte mit einer schrittweisen Übernahme der Macht auch Reformen ins Land bringen. 2013 war es dann für den Sport soweit. Laut Entscheidung des Ministerrats durften die Athleten ab Januar 2014 im Ausland Profiverträge abschließen. Boxfunktionär Alberto Puig de la Barca unterzeichnete eine Vereinbarung, die den Beitritt

von Kubas Amateurboxern zur World Series of Boxing (WSB) regelt. Die World Series besteht aus zwölf Teams, in denen Boxer in fünf Gewichtsklassen aus mehr als fünfzig Nationen antreten. Achtzig Prozent der Preisgelder sollen in die Taschen der Athleten fließen.

Was auch immer das für Stil und Trainingsweise im eigenen Land bedeuten wird, ist noch nicht ganz absehbar. Doch eines ist klar: Leistung soll sich lohnen und am Einkommen messbar werden. Womit man natürlich die großen Talente im eigenen Land halten will. Denn sie verpflichten sich dafür umgekehrt, in den einheimischen Ligen zu boxen und Kubas Nationalteam zur Verfügung zu stehen. Deshalb gilt Boxen heute mehr denn je als Traumberuf, auch wenn man sich für diesen Traum von frühester Jugend an einem harten Training unterstellen muss. Einer der Jungen, Erislandy Savón, Mitglied des Nationalkaders und Neffe der kubanischen Boxlegende Félix Savón, verbindet seine Begeisterung für den Sport mit einem

neuerwachten Lebensgefühl: »Wir Boxer bekommen einfach alles.«

Félix Savón – Kubas Boxstil wird sich ändern

Auch Félix Savón, dreifacher Olympiasieger und sechsfacher Weltmeister, einer der ganz Großen wie Stevenson, arbeitet heute als Trainer. Er ist bei den Kämpfen des Giraldo Córdova Cardín zugegen, bei denen das Jahr 2013 ebenjenen Aufbruch in eine neue Profiboxära markiert.

Savón weiß, dass die Reformen das Boxen selbst verändern werden. Im professionellen Bereich geht der Kampf über fünf Runden statt drei. Ein anderes Punktesystem bestimmt von nun an die Taktik. Bei den Amateuren zählt die Gesamtpunktzahl, weshalb manche Runde durchaus tänzelnd und ausweichend gestaltet werden kann. Im Profiboxen hingegen ist das völlig anders. Hier muss jede Runde für sich entschieden werden. Mehrere Treffer ganz ohne Kopfschutz stellen eine ganz andere Belastung dar. Das wirkt sich als Allererstes auf das Training aus, das härter werden

home cannot be entirely predicted as yet. But one thing is clear: performance should pay off and be reflected in income. At the same time, of course, the idea is to keep major prospects in the country. For they, in turn, commit to boxing in the national leagues and to being available for Cuba's national team. This is why boxing, today more than ever, is seen as a dream job, even if it means having to subject oneself to rigorous training from an early age. One of the young ones, Erislandy Savón, who is part of the national squad and a nephew of Cuban boxing legend, Félix Savón, combines his enthusiasm for the sport with a new lifestyle: "We boxers simply get everything."

Félix Savón—Cuba's Boxing Style Will Change

Félix Savón, a three-time Olympic champion, six-time world champion and, like Stevenson, one of the greatest, also works as a trainer today. He attends the fights at the Giraldo Córdova Cardín where 2013 marked the dawn of a new era of professional boxing.

Savón knows that the reforms will change boxing itself. Professional fights go five rounds rather than three. From now on a different point system determines tactics. In amateur boxing what counts is the total number of points scored, which is why individual rounds can be dominated by dancing and sidestepping. Things are completely different, though, in professional boxing, where fighters have to try to decide each round for themselves. Multiple hits without a head guard cause a very different kind of strain. First and foremost this affects training which will become more rigorous and adapt the dance-like Cuban style to the international version. Now the boxers lace up their gloves even tighter as they have become heavier.

Cuba's Special Way of Taking on the Opponent

Cuban boxing is a very special form of boxing where speed and technical perfection go hand in hand with lithe agility and elegance—"Cuba libre" or "Cuba Salsa" in its athletic form. The elegance of the moves draws on the

peculiarly Cuban attitude towards life which manages to combine work, sweat, and rigor with a sense of rhythm. Thudding punches and springy feet echo from the bare walls as opponents face one another in the ring and go at one another with their heavy fists.

La Finca—Élite Training Center for Cuba's Boxers

La Finca could be described as a tranquil place on the outskirts of Havana where salsa music dominates the day and vintage American cars from the 1940s and 1950s—metallic blue or pastel pink Cadillacs, Oldsmobiles, Chevrolets and Fords—are parked in front of people's homes, a place where the best boxers train in a relaxed atmosphere among palm and mango trees. But no—far from it.

Those who made it here still have an arduous path ahead of them, because training is rigorous and all about discipline. For the national squad this means first training sessions straight after getting up in the morning. Not one training jersey remains dry in the hot, humid Havana air. "Mural Informa-

und den tänzerischen kubanischen Stil einem internationalen angleichen wird. Die Boxer schnüren ihre schwerer gewordenen Handschuhe nun fester.

Kubas spezielle Art, dem Gegner zu begegnen

Der kubanische Boxkampf hat seine ganz spezielle Ausformung. Schnelligkeit und technische Perfektion gehen einher mit einer geschmeidigen Beweglichkeit und Eleganz. »Cuba libre« oder »Cuba Salsa« in seiner athletischen Form. Die Eleganz der Bewegungen speist sich aus jenem kubanischen Lebensgefühl, das Arbeit, Schweiß und Härte mit einem Gefühl für Rhythmus und Takt zu verbinden weiß. Dumpfe Schläge und federnde Füße hallen von den kahlen Wänden wider, wenn sich die Gegner im Ring gegenüberstehen und mit ihren schweren Fäusten aufeinander losgehen.

La Finca – Kaderschmiede für Kubas Boxer

La Finca könnte man als einen beschaulichen Ort am Rande Havannas beschreiben, wo Salsa-Musik den Tag bestimmt und US-amerikanische Oldtimer-Schlitten der Vierziger und Fünfziger, Cadillacs, Oldsmobile, Chevrolets und Fords in Metallicblau oder Pastellrosa, vor der Tür stehen. Wo die besten Kämpfer zwischen Palmen und Mangobäumen in entspanntem Ambiente trainieren. Doch weit gefehlt. Wer es bis hierhin gebracht hat, dem steht noch ein anstrengender Weg bevor, denn das Training ist hart und von Disziplin geprägt. Für das Nationalkader bedeutet das erste Trainingseinheiten direkt nach dem Aufstehen. In der schwülheißen Luft Havannas bleibt kein Trainingsshirt trocken. »Mural Informativo Boxeo« heißt die überdimensionale Pinnwand, auf der die Athleten ihrem Trainer zugeteilt werden – Gewichtseinheiten sind obligatorisch. Medaillengewinner wie Lenier Pero oder Yasniel Toledo stehen neben dem Star des Teams Roniel Iglesias Sotolongo, der 2012 in London Gold holte. In der Finca selbst wird erbrachte Leistung mit besonderen Boni belohnt. Nur die Boxelite profitiert von ihren Erfolgen mit besonderem Essen und Wohneinheiten mit Balkon, Klimaanlage und Satellitenfernsehen. Die funkelnagelneuen chinesischen Autos vor der Tür inklusive.

Trainer des Nationalkaders

Enrique Steiner ist einer der Nationaltrainer. Er beobachtet, wie sich das Kampf- und Trainingsverhalten mit Einführung des Profisportes verändert. Er lässt seine Schützlinge häufiger Laufrunden absolvieren und Gewichte stemmen. »Die Neuregelungen werden das kubanische Boxen langsamer, aber auch härter machen«, ist sein Fazit.

Ángelo Morejón hat es Ende 2012 in das kubanische Nationalkader geschafft und wird von Steiner im Halbschwergewicht noch eiserner trainiert als zuvor.

Rolando Acebal, ebenfalls Boxnationaltrainer, sieht die Entwicklung ähnlich. Er beobachtet Roniel Iglesias Sotolongo, der gerade auf seinen Gegner im Ring einschlägt. Wichtiges Training, so Acebal, um die Jungs für das Profigeschäft abzuhärten. Roniel Iglesias ist kubanischer Vorzeige-Athlet. Amtierender Olympiasieger, Welt-

...colate Quiere Decir Oro, en el Lenguaje Moderno del Pugilismo

Kid Chocolate, Karikatur
Caricature of Kid Chocolate

tivo Boxeo" is the name of the huge pin board on which the athletes are assigned their trainers—sessions involving weights are mandatory. Medalists such as Lenier Pero and Yasniel Toledo are listed next to the star of the team, Roniel Iglesias Sotolongo, who won gold in London in 2012. At the Finca itself performance is rewarded with special bonuses. Only the boxing élite benefit from their successes in the form of special food and living quarters with balcony, AC and satellite TV—including the brand spanking new Chinese cars parked outside.

Trainer of the National Squad

Enrique Steiner is one of the national trainers. He observes the ways in which fighting and training behavior is changing as a result of the introduction of professional boxing. He makes his protégés run circuits and lift weights more frequently. "The new rules will make Cuban boxing slower, but also tougher," he concludes.

Ángelo Morejón made the Cuban national squad in late 2012, and the training in light heavyweight he is subjected to by Steiner is more relentless than before.

Rolando Acebal, also a national boxing trainer, sees the development in a similar light. He is watching Roniel Iglesias Sotolongo as the latter throws punches at his opponent in the ring. Important training, Acebal says, to toughen up the guys for pro boxing. Roniel Iglesias is a model Cuban athlete. Reigning Olympic gold medalist, world champion, and multiple Pan-American champion in light welterweight up to 64 kg, he still trains with the younger and inexperienced ones, which in Cuba's élite academies is considered normal.

Acebal and Steiner keep an eye on all of them, as they scurry between the ropes of the three boxing rings. The boxing matches are held simultaneously in all weight divisions. When boxers from abroad attend training, additional makeshift rings are built.

A Training System Aimed Even at the Very Young

One reason for Cuba's exceptional success in boxing is the early promotion of talented children. Newly discovered talents are already placed in regional boxing centers at the age of nine. Roniel Iglesias Sotolongo was only nine when he started boxing and 16 when he was accepted into the intensive training center. After that his career skyrocketed.

There are about 15 regional boxing centers in Cuba. One of them, the Centro Sportivo Rafael Trejo, Trejo Gym for short, is located in Havana on Calle Cuba diagonally across from the Iglesia de la Merced. A small yellow sign is all that indicates the training areas behind. Here, too, a photograph of Kid Chocolate, who has left his mark everywhere, is hanging in the entrance. Though much seems crumbling or rusted, the place is full of life, energy, and combativeness. A lively atmosphere welcomes anyone who is admitted to this world, which is not a given. While some are still warming up or pummeling the punching bag as an imaginary opponent, others are already entering the ring. Some cold water on the face quick, then let's roll. Not an easy job for the trainers to

meister und mehrfacher panamerikanischer Meister im Halbweltergewicht bis 64 Kilogramm trainiert er trotzdem mit den Jüngeren und Unerfahrenen. Eine Selbstverständlichkeit in Kubas Eliteschulen.

Acebal und Steiner haben sie alle im Auge, während sie zwischen den Seilen der drei Boxringe hin- und hereilen. Die Kämpfe werden parallel in allen Gewichtsklassen ausgetragen. Sind Kämpfer aus dem Ausland beim Training dabei, werden provisorisch weitere Ringe aufgebaut.

Ein Trainingssystem schon für die Jüngsten

Dass Kuba so erfolgreich im Boxen ist, hat seinen Grund auch in der frühen Förderung begabter Kinder. Bereits im Alter von 9 Jahren werden die Neuentdeckungen in regionale Boxzentren gesteckt. Roniel Iglesias Sotolongo war erst neun Jahre alt, als er mit dem Boxen begann, und 16, als er ins Leistungszentrum kam. Seitdem ging seine Karriere steil bergauf.

Regionale Boxzentren gibt es in Kuba circa 15. Das Centro Sportivo Rafael Trejo zum Beispiel, Trejo Gym genannt, liegt in Havanna an der Calle Cuba schräg gegenüber der Iglesia de la Merced. Nur ein kleines gelbes Schild weist auf das Trainingsgelände dahinter. Auch hier hängt am Eingang ein Foto von »Kid Chocolate«, der überall seine Spuren hinterlassen hat. Wenngleich vieles brüchig geworden ist oder verrostet scheint, so ist der Ort voller Leben, Energie und kämpferischem Einsatz. Eine quirlige Atmosphäre empfängt jeden, der Zutritt in diese Welt erhält. Was keine Selbstverständlichkeit ist. Während sich die einen noch warm machen oder auf den Punchingball als imaginären Gegner eintrommeln, begeben sich die anderen schon in den Ring. Schnell noch kaltes Wasser ins Gesicht und auf geht's. Für die Trainer keine leichte Aufgabe, diesen boxbesessenen Ameisenhaufen unter sportlicher Kontrolle zu halten. Der Schweiß steht ihnen bereits auf der Stirn.

Boxchampions trainieren die Jüngsten in der Havana City Boxing Academy

Die Kinder, die hier nach der Schule trainieren, leben den Traum von Erfolg, Anerkennung und Reichtum. Urgestein Jorge Hernández, 1974 Weltmeister im eigenen Land und 1976 Olympiasieger in Montreal, bereitet sie auf den nächsten Kampf und ihre Gegner vor. Ramón Duvalón und Sixto Soria Cabrera, beide Vize-Olympiasieger 1976, gehören mit zum Trainingsstab. Es sind die Boxchampions, die sich mit Geduld und fachlichem Know-how um die Kleinsten bemühen.

In Havannas City Boxing Academy werden die Kinder bereits vor der Schule um vier Uhr früh aus den Federn geholt. »Man muss Opfer bringen«, so sehen das die meisten und sind eifrig und durchwegs großartig begabt beim frühen Training unterwegs. Im Schulunterricht ist die Energie entsprechend reduziert. Doch für ihre Leidenschaft nehmen die Kinder vieles in Kauf. Auch um der Armut zu entfliehen und ein Ziel im Leben zu finden. Denn Boxen ist ihr Streben nach einer besseren Zukunft, die man sich mit Kraft, Mut und Ehrgeiz erkämpfen muss.

Hoch hinaus in Olympias Athletenhimmel

Besonders glücklich schätzen dürfen sich jene, die für die großen Wettkämpfe, allen voran Olympia nominiert sind. Seit 1904 ist Boxen olympische Disziplin. Die Kämpfe starteten

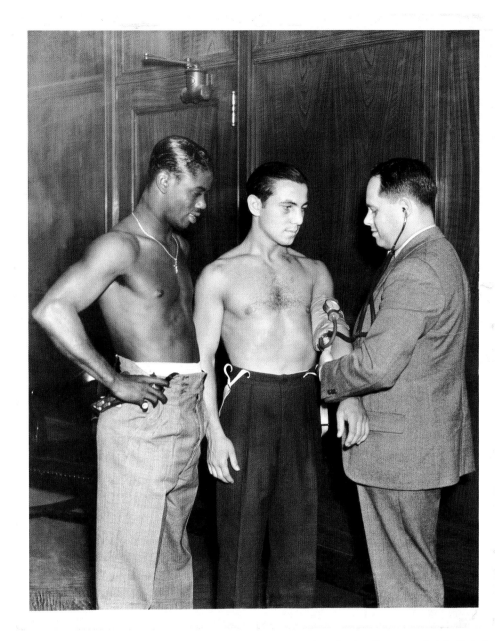

Kid Chocolate (links)
Kid Chocolate (left)

keep this anthill of boxing enthusiasts under athletic control—sweat is dripping from their foreheads already.

Boxing Champions Train the Very Young at the Havana City Boxing Academy

The children that train here after school live the dream of success, recognition, and riches. Veteran trainer Jorge Hernández, who in 1974 became world champion in his own country and in 1976 won Olympic gold in Montreal, prepares them for their next fight and their opponents. The training staff also includes Ramón Duvalón and Sixto Soria Cabrera, both silver medalists at the 1976 Olympic Games. It is the boxing champions who tend to the youngest ones with patience and technical know-how.

At Havana's City Boxing Academy the children are called from their beds as early as 4 a.m. before school. "You have to make sacrifices," most of them say, as they eagerly go about their early training, all without exception superbly talented. During school lessons their energy is reduced accordingly. Yet the children have to put up with a lot for their passion—in order to escape poverty and find a goal in life as well. For boxing is their aspiration to a better future that they must fight for with strength, courage, and ambition.

Aiming High to the Olympic Pantheon of Athletes

Those who have been nominated for the great sporting events, primarily the Olympics, can count themselves lucky. Boxing has been an Olympic discipline since 1904. At first, boxing matches were in seven weight divisions; in 2008 the number of weight classes in which boxers compete went up to eleven and in 2016 to twelve. Women, too, are now allowed to box competitively in three weight divisions at the Olympics, though for Cuba this is a non-issue: boxing remains a purely male domain. It would be a sensation if, for a change, women were allowed to compete.

Equally sensational is the decision by the AIBA with regard to the Olympic Games in Rio. Until now the rules of the international amateur boxing association (AIBA) served as the basis for boxing as an Olympic discipline. This meant that only amateur or semi-professional boxers of the World Series of Boxing and the association's own division were allowed to compete. But AIBA has lifted the restriction on

anfangs in sieben Gewichtsklassen, ab 2008 waren es elf. 2016 sind es zwölf Klassen, die antreten. Auch Frauen sind in drei Gewichtsklassen zugelassen. Für Kuba allerdings kein Thema. Hier bleibt Boxen absolute Männerdomäne. Eine Sensation wäre es, wenn auch einmal Frauen starten dürften.

Eine Sensation ist auch die Entscheidung der AIBA für die Olympischen Spiele in Rio. Bislang waren die Regeln des Weltververbandes für Amateurboxen (AIBA) Grundlage für das Boxen als olympische Disziplin. Das bedeutete, die Teilnahme war nur Amateurboxern oder semiprofessionellen Boxern der World Series of Boxing und der verbandseigenen Abteilung gestattet. Doch die AIBA hat die Beschränkung für die Teilnahme von Profis pünktlich zu den Spielen 2016 aufgehoben und das Wort »Amateur« aus ihrem Namen gestrichen. Dieses Mal dürfen auch Berufsboxer aus den bekannten Verbänden der WBA, WBC, IBF und WBO teilnehmen. Erstmals wird wieder ohne Kopfschutz gekämpft. Somit werden auch bekannte Namen aus dem Profisport bei den Olympischen Spielen zu sehen sein – doch werden die Amateure sich gegen sie behaupten können?

Den Namen Kubas würdig vertreten – Kubas Boxer in Rio 2016

Für die Boxer aus Kuba, die sich seit den Reformen Raúl Castros dem Profisport öffnen durften, eine neuerliche Änderung: Das Trainingspensum hat in den Leistungszentren, auch wenn dies kaum mehr möglich schien, noch einmal deutlich angezogen. Im Bantamgewicht tritt Lázari Álvarez bei den Olympischen Spielen in Rio an. Ganze 1,60 Meter groß und gerade mal 19 Jahre alt ist Joahnys Argilagos, der im Halbfliegengewicht startet. Yasniel Toledo aus Camagüey, Hauptstadt der gleichnamigen Provinz, und Yosvany Veitía Soto aus dem zentralkubanischen Sancti Spíritus konnten sich ebenso für die Spiele qualifizieren wie Arlen López, der beim Giraldo Córdova Cardín siegreich war und die kubanische Meisterschaft mit sieben Siegen in der Saison 2015 erkämpfte. Erislandy Savón darf als Neffe des erfolgreichen Felix Savón mit großem Namen, noch größerem Talent und ausgefeilter Technik punkten. José Larduet war bereits 2012 Teilnehmer bei den Olympischen Spielen, so wie sein kubanischer Kollege Roniel Iglesias, der mit Bronze in Peking und Gold in London der absolute Star am kubanischen Boxhimmel ist. Julio César La Cruz, der junge Robeisy Ramírez im Fliegengewicht, Odlanier Solís, Olympiasieger im Schwergewicht, und Yosvany Veitía sind alle mit in Rio. Die Hoffnungen Kubas liegen auch dieses Mal auf starken und sieggewohnten Schultern. Der Kampf um die Medaille ist auch der Kampf um Ehre und Respekt. Persönlich und für eine ganze Nation. Eine friedliche Revolution mit weltpolitischer Vision. Was könnte man mit Boxen mehr erreichen?

Kid Gavilán

the participation of pros just in time for the 2016 Olympics and removed the word "amateur" from its name. This time the professional boxers of the established associations—WBA, WBC, IBF and WBO—are allowed to compete. For the first time, Olympians will fight without head guards again. And so we will see well-known names from pro boxing at the Olympic Games as well—but will the amateurs be able to hold their ground against them?

Representing Cuba with Dignity— Cuba's Boxers at the 2016 Rio Olympics

Yet another change for the boxers from Cuba who have been allowed to go pro since the reforms of Raúl Castro: the training workload at the intensive training centers has once more been raised substantially, even if this barely seemed possible anymore. At bantamweight, Lázari Álvarez is competing in the Olympic Games in Rio. Just over five feet tall and barely 19 years old, Joahnys Argilagos is competing at light flyweight. Yasniel Toledo from Camagüey, the capital of the province of the same name, and Yosvany Veitía Soto from Sancti Spíritus in central Cuba managed to

qualify for the Olympics, as did Arlen López who was victorious at the Giraldo Córdova Cardín and won the 2015 Cuban championship with seven victories. Erislandy Savón, the nephew of Felix Savón, is allowed to score points with a big name, even bigger talent, and a refined technique. José Larduet already competed in the 2012 Olympic Games, as did his fellow Cuban, Roniel Iglesias, who won bronze in Beijing and gold in London, making him the absolute star in the

Cuban boxing pantheon. Julio César La Cruz, the young Robeisy Ramírez at flyweight, Odlanier Solís, winner of Olympic gold in heavyweight, and Yosvany Veitía are all part of the Rio team. Once again Cuba's hopes rest on strong shoulders accustomed to winning. The fight for medals is also a fight for honor and respect—both personally and for an entire nation. A peaceful revolution with a global political vision: what more could boxing achieve?

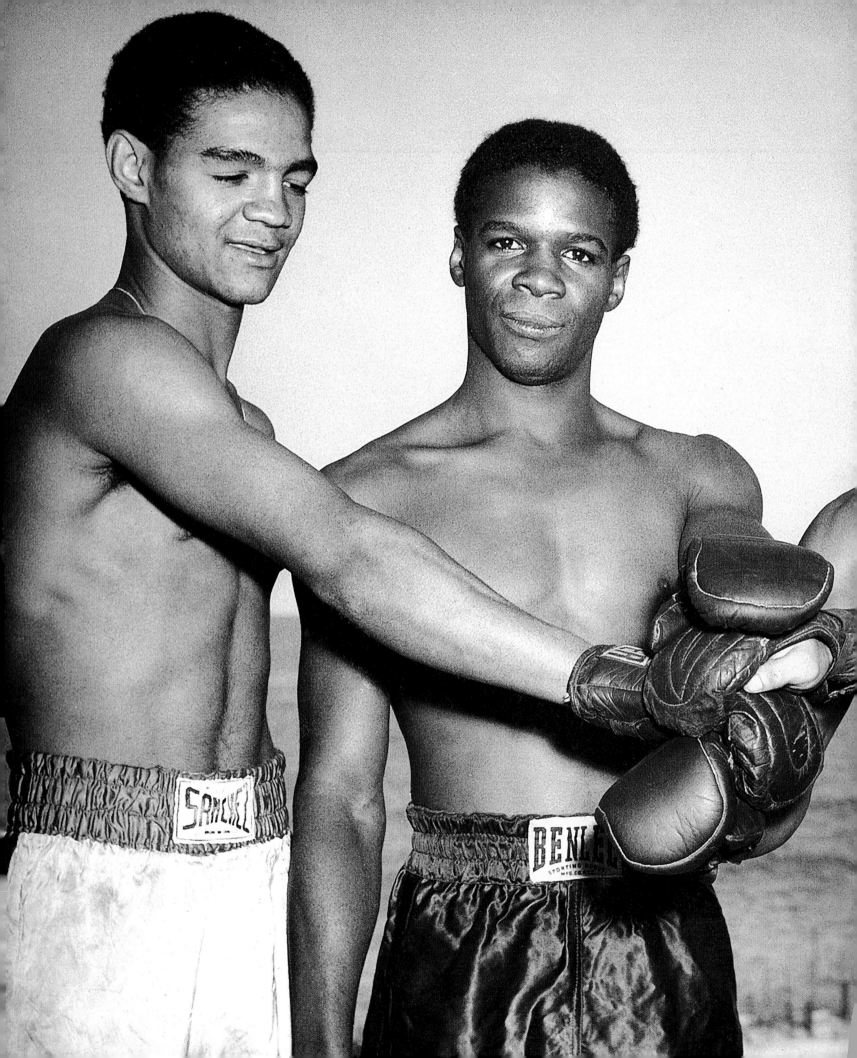

Eine kurze Geschichte des Boxens in Kuba

Aus den Erinnerungen eines Trainers

Die Anfänge

Der genaue Beginn des Boxsports in Kuba lässt sich nicht ermitteln. Ebenso wie der Baseball ist er mit dem auf der Insel herrschenden kulturellen nordamerikanischen Einfluss verknüpft. Da die Ausübung dieses Sports nicht besonders kostspielig ist, waren einfache Faustkämpfe bei den unteren Gesellschaftsklassen des Landes verbreitet, während sie innerhalb der aristokratischen Kreise in strikter organisierter Form aufgezogen wurden. Dort wurden auch Basketball und Tennis gespielt, Sportarten, für die man Ausrüstungen und Zubehör brauchte, die nur für die wohlhabenden Bevölkerungsgruppen erschwinglich waren.

Offensichtlich ist der Boxsport nach der Gründung der Republik im Jahr 1902 in der ersten Dekade des 20. Jahrhunderts aus den Vereinigten Staaten nach Kuba gekommen. Die Historiker der Zeit wie etwa der Grieche Costas Broumas berichten, dass Anfang 1900 einige Talentjäger nach Kuba kamen, um unter den schwarzen Arbeitern in den Zucker-rohrfeldern Boxer-Begabungen zu finden. Aus dem von Willy del Pino zusammengestellten Kompendium **Enciclopedia Del Boxeo Cubano** geht hervor, dass der Chilene Juan Fernando García Budinich, der in den Vereinigten Staaten Karriere als Boxer gemacht hatte, im Jahr 1910 nach Havanna kam, um seine Dienste als Personenschützer und Selbstverteidigungs-Trainer anzubieten.

Einige Monate darauf wird in der kubanischen Hauptstadt die erste Boxschule eröffnet, die samt ihrem Gründer Budinich von dem aristokratischen Vedado Tennis Club unter Vertrag genommen wird. Ziel war es, die Jugendlichen in der Kunst des Faustkampfes zu ertüchtigen, für das Boxen zu begeistern und eine größere Breitenwirkung zu erzielen. Über Budinich selbst ist sehr wenig bekannt, sein Geburtsdatum bleibt ein Geheimnis, auch ist nicht klar, wie er zum Boxen kam. Es heißt, er habe das Boxen von den englischen Marine-Soldaten gelernt.

Zu Budinichs Schülern zählten jene jungen Männer, die als Pioniere des Boxsports in Kuba gelten: Victor Achán, Tomás Galiana, Mike Febles und Bernardino San Martín. Die Kämpfe dieser ersten kubanischen Boxer hatten einen familiären oder freundschaftlichen Charakter und wurden »Fiestas« genannt, weil sie in aller Regel im Haus eines Mitglieds ihrer Gruppe oder von dessen Freunden veranstaltet wurden.

Im Lauf der Zeit wurden die Kämpfe immer populärer und es kamen immer zahlreichere Besucher zu den Veranstaltungen. Ab 1916 setzten die Tourneen der Amateurboxer von La Habana durch die Provinzen ein. In kürzester Zeit verbreitete sich der Boxsport in ganz Kuba und brachte eine Fülle von Talenten hervor. So zum Beispiel Antolín Fierro, der als der wahrer Champion im Schwergewicht angesehen wurde, oder das Fliegengewicht José García, der den besten Boxern seiner Gewichtsklasse die Stirn bot.

Dem Boxstall der Stadt Cienfuegos entstammten Enrique Ponce de León, Champion in der 147er-Pfund-Gewichtsklasse, und Generoso Pino, dem es

A Brief History of Boxing in Cuba
From the recollections of a coach

The Beginnings

The exact time when boxing originated in Cuba cannot be pinpointed. Like baseball it was linked to the cultural influence of North America that was prevalent on the island. Since practicing this sport does not involve much of an expense, bare fist fights were popular among the country's lower social classes. In aristocratic circles, by contrast, such fights were more strictly organized. Other sports played in these circles were basketball and tennis, which both required equipment and accessories that only the affluent segments of the population could afford.

Apparently, boxing came from the United States to Cuba in the first decade of the twentieth century after the founding of the Republic in 1902. According to historians of the period such as the Greek scholar Costas Broumas, a few talent scouts came to Cuba in early 1900 looking for boxing talents among the black workers in the cane fields. As the **Enciclopedia Del Boxeo Cubano**, which was compiled by Willy del Pino, informs us,

Juan Fernando García Budinich, a Chilean who had carved out a career as a boxer in the United States, came to Havana in 1910 to offer his services as a bodyguard and self-defense instructor.

A few months later, the Cuban capital saw the opening of the first boxing school which, together with its founder, Budinich, was signed on by the aristocratic Vedado Tennis Club. The aim was to train youths in the art of pugilism and to raise interest in boxing and broaden its appeal. Very little is known about Budinich himself: his date of birth remains a mystery and it is also not clear what drew him to boxing. It is said that he was taught boxing by English marines.

Among Budinich's pupils were the young men who are considered the pioneers of boxing in Cuba: Victor Achán, Tomás Galiana, Mike Febles and Bernardino San Martín. The bouts of these first Cuban boxers were of an informal or friendly nature and called "fiestas," because as a rule they were held at the home of a member of the group or of a friend of a member.

Over time the boxing matches became increasingly popular and more and more people came to attend the events. Starting in 1916, the amateur boxers from La Habana went on regular tours of the provinces. Within a very short time boxing spread throughout Cuba and spawned a wealth of talents, such as Antolín Fierro, who was regarded as the true heavyweight champion, and the flyweight, José García, who held his own against the best boxers of his weight class.

Successful boxers from the squad of the city of Cienfuegos were welterweight champion, Enrique Ponce de León, and Generoso Pino, who managed to win the belt in flyweight. Other cities produced highly skilled boxers as well. Topping the list of boxers from Sagua la Grande is Esteban Gallard a.k.a Kid Charol, a middleweight who is considered one of the best Cuban boxers of all time. Sagua la Grande produced other great boxers such as Ramón Cabrera, Roleaux Sagüero, Kid Molinet, Kid Ríos, Juan Tapia and Young Molina. In the

Sonny Leon aus Venezuela (2. v. l.)
und Puppy García (2. v. r.)
Sonny Leon from Venezuela (2nd f.l.)
and Puppy García (2nd f.r.)

gelang, den Gürtel im Fliegengewicht zu erringen. Aber auch in anderen Städten gab es hochqualifizierte Kämpfer. Die Liste der Boxer von Sagua la Grande wird angeführt von Esteban Gallard, alias »Kid Charol«, einem Mittelgewicht, der als einer der besten kubanischen Boxer aller Zeiten gilt. Ebenfalls aus Sagua la Grande kamen Kämpfer wie Ramón Cabrera, Roleaux Sagüero, »Kid Molinet«, »Kid Ríos«, Juan Tapia und Young Molina. Im Osten war Palma Soriano der Boxstandort par excellence, obgleich auch Kämpfe von hohem Niveau in Santiago de Cuba, Holguín, Guantánamo, Manzanillo, Baracoa und Jiguaní stattfanden. Zu den wichtigsten Boxern aus dem östlichen Kuba zählten Bill Scott, John Herrera und Goyito Rico.

Die Einführung des kubanischen Boxsports und der kubanische Boxverband

Die ersten Schritte zu einer Organisation des Boxsports in Kuba wurden von den Promotern Vicente Cubillas und Bernardino San Martín unternommen, die ab 1915 einem großen Publikum nach und nach die ersten öffentlich zugänglichen Boxhallen boten: den Ring Cuba und den Black Cat Ring. Zu dieser Zeit wurde auch The Stadium errichtet, die erste

lediglich dem Boxen vorbehaltene Arena. Auch im Hipódromo »Oriental Park« fanden Kämpfe statt, etwa zwischen den Schwergewichtlern Jack Johnson und Jess Willard. Ab diesem Zeitpunkt bewarben sich sogar Theaterbesitzer darum, Boxkämpfe anzusetzen.

Einen tragischen Rückschlag erlitt der Boxsport am 21. März 1918, als der kubanische Boxer Joe Marroquín durch einen Schlag seines Gegners Alex Puebles im Recreo de Belascoaín während des Kampfes verstarb. Der **alcalde** (Bürgermeister) von Havanna erklärte daraufhin die Ausübung des Boxsports für illegal: »Das Boxen ist brutal, barbarisch [...]. Solange ich Bürgermeister von Havanna bin und solange ich die Erlaubnis für diesen barbarischen Sport verweigern kann, wird es ihn nicht geben.«

Im Jahr 1921 jedoch – nach Überwindung des Widerstands durch einen neuen Bürgermeister von Havanna, Marcelino Díaz de Villegas, der die Politik des Boxsportverbots seines Vorgängers fortzusetzen suchte – entschied die **secretaría de gobernación** (Regierungssekretariat, vergleichbar mit dem deutschen Innenministerium) per Dekret die Gründung der Comisión Nacional de Boxeo y Luchas (Kommission für den Boxsport und andere Kampfsportarten), um die

Durchführung des Boxsports in Kuba zu organisieren. Am 13. Dezember 1921 wurde die Kommission schließlich dauerhaft etabliert.

Die Kommission legte Gewichtslimits innerhalb von neun Klassen fest und verkündete die ersten nationalen Champions in diesen Klassen. Sie bestimmte außerdem, dass jeder Boxer, der einen Titel innehatte, diesen innerhalb von sechs Monaten ab dem Datum des Sieges zu verteidigen hatte. Dem Boxer, der dieser Auflage nicht nachkam, wurde der Titel entzogen. Die Gürtel der verschiedenen Klassen waren Eigentum der Kommission und durften nur von den Champions benutzt werden, die verpflichtet waren, sie vor der Institution zu präsentieren, so oft diese es verlangte, und sie zurückzugeben, wenn sie den Meistertitel verloren. Auch mussten die Boxer ihre Lizenz als Profiboxer in regelmäßigen Abständen erneuern. Falls sie dieser Auflage nicht nachkamen, durften sie auf kubanischem Gebiet nicht mehr kämpfen.

Zu Beginn des folgenden Jahrzehnts schuf der Eigentümer der Zeitungen »La Noche« und »La Lucha« eine Boxschule für Kinder und Jugendliche zwischen 8 und 15 Jahren. Das Ziel war nicht nur das Boxtraining, sondern auch die Verkaufsförde-

East, Palma Soriano was a boxing location par excellence, although high-level bouts also took place in Santiago de Cuba, Holguín, Guantánamo, Manzanillo, Baracoa and Jiguaní. Among the most important boxers from Eastern Cuba were Bill Scott, John Herrera and Goyito Rico.

The Introduction of Cuban Boxing and the Cuban Boxing Association

First steps towards organized boxing in Cuba were taken by the promoters Vicente Cubillas and Bernardino San Martín who, from 1915 on, established the first boxing clubs that were accessible to the wider public: the Ring Cuba and the Black Cat Ring. Around the same time the Stadium, the first dedicated boxing arena, was built. Boxing matches were also held at the Hipódromo "Oriental Park," including a bout between heavyweights Jack Johnson and Jess Willard. From this

time on, even theater owners were eager to schedule boxing matches.

Boxing suffered a tragic setback on March 21, 1918 when the Cuban boxer Boxer Joe Marroquín died in the ring as a result of a punch by his opponent, Alex Puebles, at the Recreo de Belascoaín. After this, the **alcalde** (mayor) of Havana declared the practice of boxing illegal: "Boxing is brutal, barbaric [...]. As long as I am mayor of Havana and as long as I can deny permission for this barbaric sport, there will not be any boxing."

Yet in 1921, after overcoming the resistance of a new mayor of Havana, Marcelino Díaz de Villegas, who tried to continue his predecessor's policy of banning boxing, the **secretaría de gobernación**, or Secretariat of the Interior, decided by decree to set up the Comisión Nacional de Boxeo y Luchas (National Commission of Boxing and Wrestling), in order to

organize the practice of boxing in Cuba. On December 1921 the commission was eventually established on a permanent basis.

The commission defined weight limits within nine classes and announced the first national champions in those classes. It also determined that any boxer holding a title would have to defend this title within six months of winning it. Any boxer failing comply with this requirement would be stripped of his title. The belts of the various weight classes belonged to the commission and were to be used only by the champions, who were obliged to present them before the institution whenever asked to do so and to return them upon losing their title. Boxers also had to periodically renew their licenses as professional boxers. If they failed to meet this requirement, they were no longer allowed to box on Cuban territory.

rung seiner Blätter. Der Gewinner jedes Kampfes erhielt 25 und der Verlierer 10 Zeitungsexemplare, die sie dann auf der Straße verkaufen sollten. Der Erlös war ihr Lohn. So begannen die Kämpfe der **aficionados**, und aus dieser Talentschmiede gingen später verschiedene Champions im Profiboxen hervor. Die ungewöhnliche Idee zündete, ihr schlossen sich zu dieser Zeit zahlreiche private Clubs an, und schließlich wurde 1922 die Comisión de Boxeo de la Unión Atlética Amateurs gegründet. Der Verband war Schirmherr der bis 1926 durchgeführten Meisterschaften, bei denen zahlreiche Boxer brillierten, darunter Eligio Sardiñas »Kid Chocolate«, der wohl berühmteste professionelle Boxer Kubas, sowie »Kid Gavilán«, José »Mantequilla« Nápoles, Ultiminio Ramos, Luis Manuel Rodríguez, die aber alle mit der Zeit vom Profisport verschluckt wurden.

Ende 1926 wurde das erste Unternehmen zur kommerziellen Vermarktung des Boxsports der Insel gegründet. Doch erst 1933 entstand die United Promoters Corporation, die mit dem Handel von Boxhandschuhen und der Vermittlung und Ansetzung von Kämpfen in anderen Ländern betraut war. So setzte sich die große Maschinerie des professionellen Boxsports in Kuba in Bewegung.

Während dieses und des folgenden Jahrzehnts entstanden Trainings- und Ausbildungszentren, sogenannte »Gymnasien«, und Kampfarenen. Die bedeutendsten waren die Arenen Galathea, Colón, Polar, Comercial, Cristal, Miramar Garden, Trejo, Cuba, das Gymnasium Kid Chocolate, der Palacio de los Deportes und das Coliseo de la Ciudad Deportiva.

Auch entstand die Asociación Guantes de Oro (Verband goldene Boxhandschuhe), die sich dem Amateurboxen widmete und als Talentschmiede für den professionellen Boxsport auftrat, der bereits begann, sich als erfolgsträchtiges Geschäft zu erweisen.

Kuba lieferte dem internationalen professionellen Boxsport zahlreiche Kämpfer, unter denen vor allem »Kid Chocolate« und »Kid Gavilán« hervorstachen. Weitere Helden im bezahlten Sport dieser Epoche waren »Kid Charol«, »Relámpago Sagüero«, »Kid Tunero«, »El Niño« Valdés, »Ciro« Morasen, »La Diabla« Díaz oder »Puppy« García. Auch berühmte Trainer wie Luis Felipe »Pincho« Gutiérrez (Trainer von Eligio Sardiñas alias »Kid Chocolate«), Antolín »Chino« Gobin, Higinio Ruíz, Luis Sarría, Félix Massud oder die Brüder Manolo und Marzo Hernández brachte Kuba hervor.

In den 1920er-Jahren und bis Ende der 1950er-Jahre präsentierten die kubanischen Boxer international ihren atypischen Stil und waren imstande, sich mit den Besten der Welt auf Augenhöhe zu messen. Trotz merklichem Einfluss des nordamerikanischen Boxens zeigt sich in ihrem Stil stets die Kultur und Tradition Kubas.

Die Revolution und das Ende des Profisports

Die kubanische Revolution, die am 1. Januar 1959 siegte, veränderte die Ausübung des Boxsports im ganzen Land vollkommen. Am 4. Januar 1962 wurde das Profiboxen in Kuba verboten und fünfzig Jahre lang durfte kein kubanischer Boxer als Vertreter seines Landes an bezahlten Kämpfen teilnehmen.

Dem Amateursport half dies: Schon ab 1961 wurde dieser systematisch weiter auf- und ausgebaut. Die Boxbegeisterung erreichte die breite Masse und so wurde die Grundlage dessen gelegt, was sich im Lauf von etwa zwanzig Jahren zur weltweit anerkannten kubanischen Boxerschule entwickelte.

Das Amateurboxen selbst ist in das kubanische Sportsystem eingebunden, das aus den Bestrebungen des am 23. Februar 1961 gegründeten Nationalen Instituts für Sport, Leibserziehung und Erholung entstanden ist.

Early in the next decade the owner of the newspapers **La Noche** and **La Lucha** established a boxing academy for children and adolescents between the ages of 8 and 15. It was not just dedicated to boxing training, but also to promoting the sales of his papers: the winner of a boxing match received 25 newspaper copies and the loser 10, which they were then supposed to sell on the street. The proceeds were their pay. Thus began the boxing matches of the **aficionados** and this talent factory subsequently produced a number of champions in professional boxing. The unusual idea caught on, with a large number of private clubs following suit around this time, and eventually the Comisión de Boxeo de la Unión Atlética Amateurs was established in 1922. The association sponsored the championships which were held until 1926 and at which numerous boxers offered impressive performances, including Eligio Sardiñas a.k.a. "Kid Chocolate," probably Cuba's most famous professional boxer, as well as Kid Gavilán, José "Mantequilla" Nápoles, Ultiminio Ramos, and Luis Manuel Rodríguez, who with time all switched to professional boxing.

In late 1926, the first company dedicated to the commercial exploitation of boxing was established on the island. Yet only in 1933 the United Promoters Corporation was established, which was charged with overseeing the trade in boxing gloves and of arranging and scheduling bouts abroad. Thus the great machinery of professional boxing in Cuba clunked into life.

Over the course of this decade and the next, training centers called "gymnasiums" and boxing arenas popped up. The most important of these were the Galathea, Colón, Polar, Comercial, Cristal, Miramar Garden, Trejo and Cuba arenas, the Kid Choco-late gym, the Palacio de los Deportes and the Coliseo de la Ciudad Deportiva.

Another body that was established was the Asociación Guantes de Oro (Golden Boxing Gloves Association), which focused on amateur boxing and served as a talent factory for professional boxing, which already began to prove to be a commercially promising business.

Cuba supplied international professional boxing with numerous athletes, among whom especially Kid Chocolate and Kid Gavilán stood out. Other

— Eine kurze Geschichte des Boxens in Kuba

Kubanische Briefmarken und 1-Peso-Münze zu den
Olympmischen Spielen 1992 in Barcelona
Cuban stamps and 1 Peso coin minted for the 1992
Olympic Games in Barcelona

Kubas Erfolge bei den Amateur-weltmeisterschaften

1971 waren schon zwöf Jahre seit dem Verbot des Profiboxens vergangen, als Kuba sich als panamerikanischer Champion im Boxen während der Panamerikanischen Spiele von Cali in Kolumbien hervortat. Im folgenden Jahr, während der Olympischen Spiele von München, errangen drei Kubaner den Meistertitel in ihren jeweiligen Gewichtsklassen: Orlando Martínez im Federgewicht, Emilio Correa Bayeux im Weltergewicht und Teófilo Stevenson im Superschwergewicht. 1974 schließlich organisierte Kuba einen ersten internationalen Wettkampf und errang vor heimischer Kulisse in Havanna bei den Wettkämpfen fünf Gold-, eine Silber- und zwei Bronzemedaillen. Damals wurde noch in elf Gewichtsklassen gekämpft. Besonders traten Jorgito Hernández, der in der Gewichtsklasse von 48 Kilo über den Kenyaner Stephen Muchoki triumphierte, der relativ kleine Boxer Douglas Rodríguez, der sich mit einer verletzten Schlaghand durch die Weltmeisterschaft kämpfte und doch in jedem seiner Kämpfe siegte, hervor sowie Teófilo Stevenson, dem es gelang, sich vom Schmerz in seinem rechten Bein zu erholen und vor dem heimischen Publikum zu glänzen.

Der Internationale Boxverband legte daraufhin fest, dass die Amateurweltmeisterschaft alle vier Jahre veranstaltet werden sollte. Die zweite Meisterschaft fand 1978 in Belgrad statt. Kuba gewann fünf Titel, wobei aber nur Stevenson in der Gewichtsklasse von 81 Kilo seinen Titel verteidigen konnte.

In München 1982 errang das kubanische Team neben weiteren Medaillen den Mannschaftssieg. 1986 fand die Weltmeisterschaft dann erstmalig auf nordamerikanischem Boden statt. Reno, wo der Boxsport begeistert betrieben wurde, war die Heimat der besten Boxer der Zeit und das Ereignis markiert den Beginn der Weltkarriere einer der größten Legenden des kubanischen Boxsports: Félix Savón wurde, obwohl noch sehr jung, in die nationale Auswahl aufgenommen.

Savón besiegte alle seine Gegner in der 91er-Gewichtsklasse, obwohl es letzlich Teófilo Stevenson war, der die Haupttitel in einem seiner letzten internationalen Auftritte einheimste. Der dreifache olympische Champion präsentierte sich in der Klasse von 91 Kilo und seine Darbietung war so eindrucksvoll, dass die Veranstalter ihm die Copa Russell zusprachen, eine Trophäe, die dem vollkommensten Boxer der Weltmeisterschaft überreicht wird.

Kuba dominierte die Weltmeisterschaft in Reno mit Siegen in sieben der zwölf Gewichtsklassen. In Moskau gewannen jedoch die Sowjets 1989 einen Titel mehr. Entscheidend war dabei der Ausgang des letzten Kampfes in der Gewichtsklasse von 51 Kilo. Die Ringrichter entschieden zugunsten von Yuri Arbachakov, womit der Kubaner Pedro Orlando Reyes als Verlierer feststand. Bis heute wird diese Entscheidung unter Kubanern viel diskutiert.

Das letzte Jahrzehnt des 20. Jahrhunderts begann für das kubanische Boxen mit einem Fragezeichen. Nach der Abwesenheit bei den Olympischen Spielen in Los Angeles und Seoul und dem umstrittenen Urteil in Moskau stellte man sich die Frage, ob die kubanischen Boxer wieder auf die ersten Plätze zurückkehren würden. Diese wurde bei der Weltmeisterschaft in Sydney 1991 eindeutig beantwortet. Die Kubaner errangen mit neun Medaillen wieder den Mannschaftssieg. Darauf folgten die Olympischen Spiele in Barcelona 1992, und hier erreichte das kubanische Boxen seinen Höhepunkt mit sieben olympischen Goldmedaillen. Auch aus diesem Grund ging die nationale Auswahlmannschaft als großer Favorit in die Weltmeisterschaft 1993 in Tamperes, Finnland. Die Kubaner lieferten hier

professional boxing heroes of this era were Kid Charol, Relámpago Sagüero, Kid Tunero, "El Niño" Valdés, "Ciro" Morasen, "La Diabla" Díaz and "Puppy" García. And Cuba also produced famous trainers such as Luis Felipe "Pincho" Gutiérrez (trainer of Kid Chocolate), Antolín "Chino" Gobin, Higinio Ruíz, Luis Sarría, Félix Massud the brothers Manolo and Marzo Hernández.

In the 1920s and through to the late 1950s, the Cuban boxers presented their atypical style internationally and were able to compete on equal footing with the best in the world. Despite the noticeable influence of North American boxing, their style continues to reflect the culture and tradition of Cuba.

The Revolution and the End of Professional Boxing

Victorious on January 1, 1959, the Cuban Revolution completely changed the practice of boxing throughout the country. On January 4, 1962 professional boxing was banned in Cuba and for half a century no Cuban boxer was allowed to participate in paid bouts as a representative of his country.

The ban bolstered amateur boxing which, starting as early as 1961, was systematically promoted and expanded. Enthusiasm for boxing spread to the mainstream and thus the founda-tion was laid of what — over the course of about twenty years — developed into the globally recognized Cuban school of boxing.

Amateur boxing itself is integrated into the Cuban sports system that grew out of the efforts of the National Institute of Sports, Physical Education and Recreation, which was founded on February 23, 1961.

Cuba's Success at Amateur World Championships

By 1971, twelve years had already passed since the ban on professional boxing, when Cuba made its mark as Pan American boxing champion at the Pan American Games in Cali, Colombia. The following year, three Cubans won gold in their respective weight classes at the Summer Olympics in Munich: Orlando Martínez in feather-weight, Emilio Correa Bayeux in welterweight and Teófilo Stevenson in super heavyweight. In 1974, Cuba finally hosted an international tourna-ment: at the contests before a home audience in Havana it won five gold, one silver and two bronze medals. At the time boxers still competed in eleven weight classes. Among those who stood out were Jorgito Hernández who prevailed over Stephen Muchoki from Kenya in light flyweight, the rela-tively short boxer Douglas Rodríguez who boxed his way to the world cham-pionship with an injured hand, win-ning each of his bouts, as well as Teófilo Stevenson who managed to recover from the pain in his right leg and shine in front of a home crowd.

The International Boxing Associa-tion subsequently declared that the amateur world championships were to be held every four years. The second World Championships took place in Belgrade in 1978. Cuba won five titles, with only Stevenson successfully defending his heavyweight title.

In Munich in 1982, the Cuban squad won the team title as well as additional medals. In 1986, the World Championships were for the first time held in North America. A hotbed of enthusiasm for boxing, Reno, Nevada, was home to the best boxers of the day and the event marked the beginning of the international career of one of the greatest legends of Cuban boxing: though still very young, Félix Savón was included in the national selection.

Savón defeated all his opponents in heavyweight, even though in the end it was Teófilo Stevenson who claimed the main titles at one of his final interna-tional appearances. The three-time Olympic champion competed in super heavyweight and his performance was so impressive that the organizers presented him with the Copa Russell,

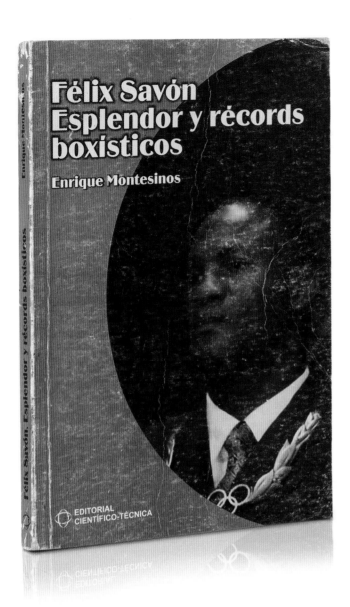

Enrique Montesinos, *Félix Savón. Esplendor y récords boxísticos*. Editorial Científico-Técnica, 2013

ihre wohl beste Vorstellung aller Zeiten: Elf der zwölf Kämpfer gelangten bis in das Finale, und acht von ihnen gewannen einen Titel. Niemals zuvor hatte ein Team eine solche Quote für sich erkämpft.

In Tamperes stiegen Félix Savón zum vierten Mal in Folge und Roberto Balado zum dritten Mal auf das Siegerpodest der Weltmeisterschaft. Auch Héctor Vinent in der Gewichtsklasse von 63,5 Kilo und Ariel Hernández mit 75 Kilo wiederholten siegreich die olympischen Erfolge von Barcelona.

Die Weltmeisterschaft von Berlin 1995 war für Kuba ein Rückschlag.

Roberto Balado war kurz zuvor bei einem Autounfall ums Leben gekommen und der Blick auf den Medaillenspiegel zeigt, dass sich in den ersten fünf Gewichtsklassen von 48, 51, 54, 57 und 60 Kilo kein einziger Kubaner für das große Finale platzieren konnte. Ab der Klasse von 63,5 Kilo änderte sich dies jedoch mit dem Triumph des Boxstars Héctor Vinent sowie dem zweiten Sieg von Juan Hernández Sierra in der Klasse von 67 Kilo. Ariel Hernández konnte zudem in der Gewichtsklasse von 75 Kilo den Siegeszug fortsetzen und an den Titel von Félix Savón von 1991 anknüpfen.

Die Medaillenausbeute war weit von der in Tampere erreichten entfernt, aber niemand wagte zu diesem Zeitpunkt, von einem Niedergang zu sprechen, insbesondere angesichts der Tatsache, dass ein Jahr später, bei der Olympiade in Atlanta, das kubanische Boxen mit weiteren vier goldenen Auszeichnungen erneut den ersten Platz belegte.

Auch weiterhin bleibt Kuba erfolgreich bei den Weltmeisterschaften und den Olympischen Spielen. Savón errang Siege bei der Weltmeisterschaft in Budapest und 2000 bei der Olympiade in Sydney, wo er auf Michael Barret

a trophy awarded to the most accomplished boxer at the world championships.

Cuba dominated the World Championships in Reno with wins in seven of the eleven weight divisions. In Moscow in 1989, however, the Soviets came out ahead of the Cubans by one title. The outcome of the final match in flyweight was crucial. The referee decided in favor of Yuri Arbachakov, handing out the loss to Pedro Orlando Reyes from Cuba — a decision that is still much-debated among Cubans to this day.

The last decade of the twentieth century began with doubts about Cuban boxing. After failing to participate in the Olympic Games in Los Angeles and Seoul and the controversial decision in Moscow it was unclear whether the Cuban boxers would be able to return to the top. All these doubts were dispelled with an impressive performance at the 1991 World Championships in Sydney. Winning a total of nine medals, the Cubans again took home the team title. This was followed by the 1992 Olympics in Barcelona where Cuban boxing peaked, claiming seven Olympic gold medals. Consequently, the national selection was a heavy favorite going into the 1993 World Championships in Tampere, Finland. There the

Cubans offered what was probably their best performance ever: eleven of the twelve boxers made it all the way to the finals and eight of them won a title. Never before had a team achieved such a success rate.

In Tampere, Félix Savón climbed on the winners' podium for the fourth time in a row and Roberto Balado for the third time in a row. Héctor Vinent in light welterweight and Ariel Hernández in middleweight also repeated their victories from the previous year in Barcelona.

The 1995 World Championships in Berlin were a setback for Cuba. Roberto Balado had recently died in a car accident and a look at the medal count shows that not one Cuban qualified for the final matches in the first five weight classes, light flyweight, flyweight, bantamweight, featherweight and lightweight. This changed, however, starting with the win of boxing star Héctor Vinent in light welterweight and the second victory of Juan Hernández Sierra in welterweight. On top of this, Ariel Hernández was able to continue his triumph in middleweight and regain Félix Savón's 1991 title.

Cuba's medal haul was a far cry from that in Tampere, but no one dared to speak of a decline at this time, especially in view of the fact that

a year later, at the 1996 Olympic Games in Atlanta, Cuban boxing once again took first place with four gold medals.

Cuba continues to be successful at World Championships and Olympic Games. Savón won titles at the World Championships in Budapest and at the 2000 Summer Games in Sydney where he faced Michael Barret. With this triumph he won his third Olympic gold medal, once again confirming that he is among the greatest stars of boxing. To date only two other boxers have managed to win Olympic gold three times: Teófilo Stevenson and Lázsló Papp from Hungary.

The first World Boxing Championships of the twenty-first century took place in Belfast, Northern Ireland, in 2001 and Cuba again experienced great moments like in the previous decade, as it won seven gold medals, including a third title for Mario Kindelán in lightweight. Two years later, in Bangkok, Thailand, the Cuban boxers won five medals, though they ceded the team title for the third time, in this case to Russia. Yet in Mianyang, China, the Cuban national team won back the overall title with a clear lead over Russia. Cuba did not attend the next World Championships which were held in Chicago in 2007. At the World Championships in Milan,

traf. Mit diesem Sieg gewann er seine dritte olympische Goldmedaille und bestätigte erneut, dass er zu den größten Stars des Boxsports zählt. Nur zwei weiteren Boxern gelang es bisher, sich dreimal Gold zu erkämpfen: Teófilo Stevenson und dem Ungaren Lázsló Papp.

Die erste Boxweltmeisterschaft des 21. Jahrhunderts fand 2001 im irischen Belfast statt, und Kuba erlebte mit sieben Goldmedaillen große Momente wie in der vorhergehenden Dekade, darunter auch die dritte für Mario Kindelán in der Gewichtsklasse von 60 Kilo. Zwei Jahre später, im thailändischen Bangkok, errangen die kubanischen Boxer fünf Medaillen, mussten aber zum dritten Mal den Mannschaftstitel abgeben, den diesmal Russland für sich beanspruchen konnte. Doch in der chinesischen Stadt Mianyang erkämpfte sich die kubanische Nationalmannschaft den Gesamtsieg mit klarem Vorsprung vor Russland zurück. Es folgte die Weltmeisterschaft in Chicago 2007, an der Kuba nicht teilnahm. Bei den Weltmeisterschaften in Mailand, Baku und Almaty errang Kuba zwar Einzelerfolge, konnte jedoch nicht mehr den Medaillenspiegel anführen. Erst bei der letzten Austragung 2015 in Doha fand Kuba mit insgesamt sieben Medaillen und dem ersten Platz im Medaillenspiegel zu alter Klasse zurück.

Über vierzig Jahre nach dem ersten Kampf um die Weltmeisterschaft ragen somit zwei Kubaner als die Gewinner der meisten Titel hervor: Félix Savón behauptet die Führung mit sechs Titeln, gefolgt von Juan Hernández Sierra mit vier Titeln. Der kubanische Boxsport hat in den zurückliegenden Weltmeisterschaften intensive und emotionale Momente nicht ohne manche Kontroversen erlebt. Siege und Enttäuschungen sind dabei stets eng mit den unvergesslichen Persönlichkeiten im Ring wie etwa Félix Savón, Teófilo Stevenson, Juan Hernández Sierra, Mario Kindelán und Roberto Balado verknüpft. Gemeinsam prägen sie alle die Geschichte kubanischen Boxsports.

Baku and Almaty Cuba posted individual wins, but was no longer able to finish at the top of the medal count. Cuba only returned to its previous dominance at the most recent championships in Doha in 2015, winning seven medals and topping the medal table.

More than forty years after the first World Championship tournament, two Cubans stand out as holding the most titles: Félix Savón maintains the lead with six titles, followed by Juan Hernández Sierra with four. At the World Championships of the recent past, Cuban boxing has experienced intense and emotional moments, some also controversial. Victories and disappointments are always closely linked to the unforgettable individuals in the ring, such as Félix Savón, Teófilo Stevenson, Juan Hernández Sierra, Mario Kindelán and Roberto Balado. Together, they are all formative for the history of Cuban boxing.

Simon Gehrke,
Teófilo Stevenson vs. Angel Milian 1979, 2016

BOXWERK

173

Michael Timm
Deutscher Trainer
German Coach

Der Chemiepokal in Halle

Training mag die eine Seite sein, doch nur durch Wettkämpfe gelangen Boxer auf das richtige sportliche Niveau, um bei Großveranstaltungen wie den Olympischen Spielen oder Weltmeisterschaften im Ring bestehen zu können. Um den Amateurboxsport zu fördern, wurden daher in den Sechzigerjahren verstärkt Turniere abgehalten, auch um einen besseren internationalen Vergleich möglich zu machen. Der Boxverein SC Chemie Halle folgte diesem Ansatz und veranstaltete, gefördert durch den Staat DDR, der bemüht war, durch sportliche Leistungen Ansehen zu erlangen, am 5. August 1970 das erste internationale Boxturnier in Halle. 82 Boxer aus 10 Nationen kämpften um den Chemiepokal, der seinen Namen der damals in der Region angesiedelten chemischen Industrie verdankt.

Mit der Wiedervereinigung 1989 fiel der staatliche Träger weg und so mussten Sponsoren für den Pokal gefunden werden, was in manchen Jahren nicht leicht war. Mit dem KSC Halle 08 fanden der Deutsche Boxsport-Verband und der Landes-Amateur-Box-Verband Sachsen-Anhalt schließlich 2010 einen neuen Ausrichter, der sich um die Weiterführung und -entwicklung des traditionsreichen Turniers kümmert.

Der Chemiepokal ist seit jeher eine Bühne für die besten und erfolgreichsten Amateurboxer, auch aus sozialistischen Staaten wie Kuba, deren Boxer den Sport bis vor wenigen Jahren nicht professionell ausüben durften. So finden sich unter den Siegern des Pokals unter anderen folgende kubanische Athleten: Joel Casamayor (olympisches Gold im Bantamgewicht 1992 in Barcelona),

Ariel Hernández (olympisches Gold im Mittelgewicht 1992 in Barcelona und 1996 in Atlanta), Mario Kindelán (olympisches Gold im Leichtgewicht 2000 in Sydney und 2004 in Athen), Guillermo Rigondeaux (olympisches Gold im Bantamgewicht 2000 in Sydney und 2004 in Athen), Félix Savón (olympisches Gold im Schwergewicht 1992 in Barcelona, 1996 in Atlanta und 2000 in Sydney) und Teófilo Stevenson (olympisches Gold im Schwergewicht 1972 in München, 1976 in Montreal und 1980 in Moskau). Doch auch weitere Berühmtheiten wie Henry Maske, Sven Ottke, Dariusz Michalczewski, Axel Schulz oder Vitali Klitschko gingen siegreich aus dem Turnier hervor und so lockt der Chemiepokal jedes Jahr Amateurboxer aus aller Welt nach Halle in die Erdgas Sportarena und zeigt einen Blick in die Zukunft des Sports.

Training während des
Chemiepokals 2016, Halle
Training during the
Chemiepokal 2016, Halle

The Chemiepokal in Halle

Training may be part of it, but it is only through actual matches that boxers achieve the right athletic level to be able to hold their own in the ring at major events such as the Olympic Games or the world championships. Hence an increasing number of tournaments were organized in the 1960s to promote amateur boxing and create better opportunities for international comparison. Following this approach, the SC Chemie Halle boxing club — with support from the government of the GDR, which strove to gain prestige through athletic accomplishments — held the first international boxing tournament in Halle on August 5, 1970. Eighty-two boxers from ten countries competed for the Chemiepokal Cup, which owes its name to the chemical industry that was located in the region at the time.

In the wake of German reunification in 1989 state support discontinued. This made it necessary to find sponsors for the cup, which in some years proved to be not easy. In 2010 the German Boxing Federation (Deutsche Boxsport-Verband) and the Amateur Boxing Association of the State of Saxony-Anhalt finally found a new host in the sports club KSC Halle 08, which now sees to the continuation and further development of the long-standing tournament.

The Chemiepokal has always been a stage for the best and most successful amateur boxers, including from socialist countries such as Cuba, whose boxers were not allowed to pursue a professional career in their sport until just a few years ago. Among the winners of the cup are the following Cuban athletes: Joel Casamayor (gold medal in bantamweight at the 1992 Summer Games in Barcelona), Ariel Hernández (gold medal in middleweight in Barcelona in 1992 and in Atlanta in 1996), Mario Kindelán (gold medal in lightweight at the 2000 Summer Games in Sydney and at the 2004 Games in Athens), Guillermo Rigondeaux (gold medal in bantamweight in Sydney in 2000 and in Athens 2004), Félix Savón (gold medal in heavyweight in Barcelona in 1992, in Atlanta in 1996 and in Sydney in 2000) and Teófilo Stevenson (gold medal in heavyweight in Munich in 1972, in Montreal in 1976 and in Moscow in 1980). Other illustrious boxers such as Henry Maske, Sven Ottke, Dariusz Michalczewski, Axel Schulz and Vitali Klitschko have won the tournament as well and so each year the Chemiepokal attracts amateur boxers from all over the world to the Erdgas Sportarena in Halle, thereby offering a glimpse of the sport's future.

Die deutsche Nationalmannschaft, 2016 in Halle / The German national team, 2016 in Halle
Hinten, von links nach rechts / in the back from left to right: Sharafa Raman, Hamza Touba, Serge Michel, Xhek Pascali, Alberto Mustafi,
Christos Cherakis, Leon Bunn, Araik Marutjan, Atdhe Gashi, Abass Baraou, Kastriot Sopa, Edison Zani
Vorne, von links nach rechts / in the front from left to right: Igor Teziev, Erik Pfeifer, Edgar Walth, Ronny Beblik, Robert Harutyunyan,
Denis Radovan, Albon Pervizaj

— Endnoten | Endnotes

Kunst und K. o.

1   A. J. Liebling, Die artige Kunst, Berlin 2009, S. 10.
2   Wolf Wondratschek, Im Dickicht der Fäuste, 2. Aufl. München 2005, S. 54.
3   Ebd., S. 53.
4   A. J. Liebling, Die artige Kunst, Berlin 2009, S. 9.
5   Vinzenz Brinkmann (Hg.), Zurück zur Klassik, München 2013, S. 330.
6   Paul Zanker, Der Boxer, in: Luca Giuliani (Hg.), Meisterwerke der antiken Kunst, München 2005, S. 29–49, hier S. 30.
7   Vinzenz Brinkmann (Hg.), Zurück zur Klassik, München 2013, S. 330.
8   Edilberto Formigli, Die Oberflächengestaltung antiker Großbronzen, in: Vinzenz Brinkmann (Hg.), Zurück zur Klassik, München 2013, S. 275–288, hier S. 286.
9   Karl-Wilhelm Weeber, Panem et circenses, Düsseldorf 1983, S. 134.
10   Max Schmeling, Erinnerungen, Frankfurt a. M./Berlin/Wien 1977, S. 87.
11   Ebd., S. 88.
12   Alfred Flechtheim, »Nun mal Schluß mit den blauen Picassos!«. Gesammelte Schriften, 2. Aufl. Bonn 2013, S. 215.
13   Anne Fleig, Körperkultur und Moderne, Berlin/New York 2008, S. 113.
14   Max Schmeling, Erinnerungen, Frankfurt a. M./Berlin/Wien 1977, S. 87.
15   Alfred Flechtheim, »Nun mal Schluß mit den blauen Picassos!«. Gesammelte Schriften, 2. Aufl. Bonn 2013, S. 14.
16   Max Schmeling, Erinnerungen, Frankfurt a. M./Berlin/Wien 1977, S. 89.
17   Ebd., S. 91.
18   Ebd., S. 94.
19   Ebd.
20   Bertolt Brecht, Gesammelte Werke 2. Stücke 2, Frankfurt a. M. 1990, S. 532.
21   Ders., Gesammelte Werke 20. Schriften zu Politik und Gesellschaft, Frankfurt a. M. 1990, S. 27.
22   Ebd., S. 28.
23   Ebd., S. 29.
24   A. J. Liebling, Die artige Kunst, Berlin 2009, S. 12.
25   Martin Krauß, Faustkampf, feinsinnig, in: http://www.taz.de/!5194029/ [gelesen am 27.1.2016].
26   O. A.: Wem die Stunde schlägt, in: Der Spiegel, 29, 1961, S. 45–52, hier S. 46.
27   Alexander Kluge / Wolf Wondratschek, Im Dickicht der Fäuste, in: http://www.dctp.tv/filme/im-dickicht-der-faeuste [gelesen am 27.1.2016].
28   Wolf Wondratschek, Im Dickicht der Fäuste, 2. Aufl. München 2005, S. 57.
29   A. J. Liebling, Die artige Kunst, Berlin 2009, S. 11.
30   Joyce Carol Oates, Über Boxen, Zürich 2013, S. 51.
31   Manfred Fuhrmann (Hg.), Aristoteles: Poetik, Stuttgart 1997, S. 19.
32   Norman Mailer, Ego, in: Life, 19.3.1971, S. 18–36, hier S. 18.
33   Ebd.
34   Ebd., S. 19.
35   Michael Schleicher, WOSH – World of Superheroes, CFM-Katalog, München 1999, S. 5.
36   Thomas Sieck, Der Zeitgeist der Superhelden, Meitingen 1999, S. 11.
37   Albert Uderzo / René Goscinny, Asterix bei den Olympischen Spielen, Stuttgart 1972, S. 40.
38   Juan Díaz Canales / Juanjo Guarnido, Blacksad, Bd. 1, Hamburg 2001, S. 11.
39   Martin Krauß, Boxen im KZ, in: Reinhard Kleist, Der Boxer, Hamburg 2012, S. 185–193, hier S. 185.
40   Joyce Carol Oates, Über Boxen, Zürich 2013, S. 23.
41   Ebd., S. 10.
42   Ebd., S. 17.
43   Ebd.
44   John E. Oden, Life in the Ring, New York 2009, S. XII.
45   Davide Enia, So auf Erden, Berlin 2014, S. 372.
46   Hans-Joachim Noack, Mann am Boden – jutet Jefühl, in: Der Spiegel, 4, 1989, S. 160–166, hier S. 166.

Porträt und Milieu

1   Einen eindrucksvollen Überblick gibt die Madeleine P. Plonsker Collection of Contemporary Cuban Photography mit der Publikation The Light in Cuban Eyes, Chicago 2014. Die Ausstellung dazu eröffnete die Robert Mann Gallery in New York am 25. März 2015.
2   Loïc Wacquant, Leben für den Ring. Boxen im amerikanischen Ghetto, Konstanz 2003.
3   »Ein System der gezielten Weiterenwicklung durch konstante, professionelle Förderung der hier trainierenden Talente zu nutzen, um die Ziele dieser Einrichtung und das Programm der Revolution zu verwirklichen.«
4   Peter Sloterdijk, Du mußt dein Leben ändern. Über Anthropotechnik, Frankfurt am Main 2009, S. 247.
5   Zitiert nach Arnd Schneider, Eine Anthropologie des Verlassenseins: Kunstethnografien in neueren Arbeiten Cyrill Lachauers, in: Ricochet #9. Cyrill Lachauer. Full Service, hg. von Michael Buhrs und Anna Schneider (Ausst.-Kat. Villa Stuck, München), Bielefeld 2015, S. 67.

Art and Knockout

1   A.J. Liebling, The Sweet Science (New York, 2004), p. 4.
2   Wolf Wondratschek, Im Dickicht der Fäuste (Munich, 2nd edn., 2005). p. 54.
3   Ibid., p. 53
4   Liebling (see note 1), p. 3.
5   Vinzenz Brinkmann (ed.), Zurück zur Klassik (Munich, 2013), p. 330.
6   Paul Zanker, "Der Boxer," in Luca Giuliani (ed.), Meisterwerke der antiken Kunst (Munich, 2005), pp. 29–49, here p. 30.
7   Brinkmann (see note 5), p. 330.
8   Edilberto Formigli, "Die Oberflächengestaltung antiker Großbronzen" in Brinkmann (see note 5), pp. 275–88, here p. 286.
9   Lucilius, "Epigrams," trans. Humbert Wolfe, in Robert Hedin and Michael Waters (eds.), Perfect in their Art: Poems on Boxing from Homer to Ali (Carbondale, IL, 2003), p. 130.
10   Max Schmeling, Erinnerungen (Berlin, 1977), p. 87.
11   Ibid., p. 88.
12   Alfred Flechtheim, "Nun mal Schluß mit den blauen Picassos!" in Flechtheim, Gesammelte Schriften (Bonn, 2nd edn., 2013), p. 215.
13   Anne Fleig, Körperkultur und Moderne (Berlin and New York, 2008), p. 113.
14   Schmeling (see note 10), p. 87.
15   Flechtheim (see note 12), p. 14.
16   Schmeling (see note 10), p. 89.
17   Ibid., p. 91.
18   Ibid., p. 94.
19   Ibid.
20   Ronald Gray, Brecht: the Dramatist (London, New York and Melbourne, 1976), pp. 38–39.
21   Bertolt Brecht, Gesammelte Werke, vol. 20: Schriften zu Politik und Gesellschaft (Frankfurt am Main, 1990), p. 27.
22   Ibid., p. 28.
23   Ibid., p. 29.
24   Liebling (see note 1), p. 6.
25   Martin Krauß, "Faustkampf, feinsinnig" in http://www.taz.de/!5194029/ (accessed January 27, 2016).
26   Martin Krauß, "Wem die Stunde schlägt," in Der Spiegel, 29 (1961), pp. 45–52, here p. 46.
27   Alexander Kluge and Wolf Wondratschek, Im Dickicht der Fäuste, http://www.dctp.tv/filme/im-dickicht-der-faeuste (accessed January 27, 2016).
28   Wondratschek (see note 2), p. 57.
29   Liebling (see note 1), p. 5.
30   Joyce Carol Oates, On Boxing (New York, 2006), p. 50.
31   Aristotle, Poetics (London, 1997), p. 19.
32   Norman Mailer, "Ego," in Life, March 19, 1971, pp. 18–36, here p. 18.
33   Ibid.
34   Ibid., p. 19.
35   Michael Schleicher, WOSH – World of Superheroes, CFM catalog (Munich, 1999), p. 5.
36   Thomas Sieck, Der Zeitgeist der Superhelden (Meitingen, 1999), p. 11.
37   Albert Uderzo and René Goscinny, Asterix at the Olympic Games (Leicester, 1972), p. 40.
38   Juan Díaz Canales and Juanjo Guarnido, Blacksad, vol. 1 (New York, 2003), p. 11.
39   Martin Krauss, "Boxen im KZ," in Reinhard Kleist, Der Boxer (Hamburg, 2012), pp. 185–93, here p. 185.
40   Oates (see note 30), pp. 18–19.
41   Ibid., p. 4.
42   Ibid., p. 11.
43   Ibid.
44   John E. Oden, Life in the Ring (New York, 2009), p. XII.
45   Davide Enia, On Earth As It Is in Heaven (New York, 2014), p. 301.
46   Hans-Joachim Noack, "Mann am Boden – jutet Jefühl," in Der Spiegel, 4 (1989), pp. 160–66, here p. 166.

Portrait and Milieu

1   An impressive survey is provided by a publication of the Madeleine P. Plonsker Collection of Contemporary Cuban Photography in a volume titled The Light in Cuban Eyes (Chicago, 2014). The accompanying exhibition opened on March 25, 2015 at the Robert Mann Gallery in New York.
2   Loïc Wacquant, Body and Soul: Notebooks of an Apprentice Boxer (New York and London: Oxford University Press, 2004).
3   "Using a system of improvement aimed at continuous, professional training of human resources to meet the objectives of this institution and comply with the program of the revolution."
4   Peter Sloterdijk, You Must Change Your Life, trans. Wieland Hoban (Cambridge and Malden, MA: Polity Press, 2013), p. 273.
5   Quoted by Arnd Schneider, "An Anthropology of Abandon: Art Ethnography in Recent Works by Cyrill Lachauer" in Michael Buhrs and Anna Schneider (eds.) in Ricochet #9. Cyrill Lachauer. Full Service, exh. cat. Villa Stuck, Munich (Bielefeld: Kerber Verlag, 2015), pp. 67.

Katharina Alt

wurde am 1. Januar 1980 in Frankfurt am Main geboren. Ihr Einstieg in die Fotografie begann 2002 bei Fotodesign Mühlensiep in Neu-Ulm. 2003 ging sie an die Hochschule München und studierte Fotodesign mit den Schwerpunkten Porträt und Reportage. Für ihr erstes großes Fotoreportageprojekt reiste sie 2005 für sechs Monate nach Kalkutta in Indien und porträtierte dort Menschen aus der unteren Arbeiterschicht. 2007 fotografierte sie in der Ostslowakei zum Thema Roma für ihr Diplom mit dem Titel **Roma 20 mm**. Seit ihrem Diplomabschluss arbeitet sie für internationale Magazine und Zeitungen. Am 18. Dezember 2014 veröffentlichte die Süddeutsche Zeitung ihr Projekt **Lebenslinien statt Falten**, in dem sie sich mit Menschen jenseits der Hundert beschäftigt. Es folgten der BR mit einem Kurzporträt über ihre Arbeit im Januar 2015 und ein Interview in der Radiosendung **Eins zu Eins. Der Talk** des BR2 im September 2015. Katharina Alt lebt und arbeitet als Fotokünstlerin in München.

was born in Frankfurt am Main on January 1, 1980. In 2002, she took her first steps in photography at Fotodesign Mühlensiep in Neu-Ulm. In 2003, she went on to attend the Munich University of Applied Science where she studied photo design with a focus on portrait and reportage. In 2005, she traveled to Kolkata, India for her first major photo reportage project: over a period of six months she portrayed working class people. In 2007 she photographed Romani people in Eastern Slovakia for her final project titled **Roma 20 mm**. Since graduating, she has been been working for international magazines and newspapers. On December 18, 2014 the **Süddeutsche Zeitung** published her project "Lebenslinien statt Falten" (Life Lines rather than Wrinkles), focusing on people who are over hundred years old. In January 2015, the Bayerischer Rundfunk (BR) did a short profile of her work and in September 2015 she was interviewed on the BR2 radio program **Eins zu Eins. Der Talk**. Katharina Alt lives and works as an photographer-artist in Munich.

— Dank | Acknowledgement

Katharina Alt

Ich bedanke mich bei Michael Schleicher, der dieses Buch mit seinem wunderbaren Text vollkommen macht. Thomas Zuhr danke ich für sein großes Vertrauen in meine künstlerische Arbeit und die Verwirklichung dieses Projekts. Ein Hoch auf das ganze Team des Hirmer Verlags für seinen Einsatz. Mein Dank gilt Christine Kron und dem Team vom Museum Fünf Kontinente, ohne die die Ausstellung nicht möglich gewesen wäre. Ebenso geht mein Dank an Petra Giloy-Hirtz, eine bessere Kuratorin kann man sich nicht wünschen. Ein großes Dankeschön an Nick Trachte, Chef des Münchner Boxwerks, für seine Ideen und sein großes Engagement. Güzin Dogan danke ich für ihre hilfreiche Inspiration. Hans Deumling für seine Zeit und sein konstruktives Feedback. Isabel Rengstorf, Samuel Puente und Miranda, die »Schlüssel« meiner Arbeit. Danke, dass ihr mich so unterstützt habt. Mein besonderer Dank geht an Peter. Dein Stolz, Deine Liebe und Deine Unterstützung lassen mein Herz jubeln.

I would like to thank Michael Schleicher for his wonderful essay, which makes this volume perfect. I thank Thomas Zuhr for his great confidence in my artistic work and for making this project a reality. I am grateful to the entire team of Hirmer Verlag for its dedication. Without Christine Kron and her team of the Museum Fünf Kontinente the exhibition would not have been possible—thank you for your support. I would also like to thank Petra Giloy-Hirtz: I couldn't have asked for a better curator. Many thanks to Nick Trachte, manager of the Boxwerk boxing gym in Munich, for his ideas and his great commitment. My thanks to Güzin Dogan for her helpful inspiration; to Hans Deumling for his time and constructive feedback; to Isabel Rengstorf, Samuel Puente and Miranda, who have been key to my work: thank you for all your support. I would like to give special thanks to Peter: your proudness, love and support make my heart rejoice.

Michael Schleicher

Ich danke Katharina Alt, ohne deren großartige Fotografien es dieses Buch nicht geben würde; Thomas Zuhr für die Bereitschaft, sich auf das Projekt einzulassen, für seinen Enthusiasmus und seine Anregungen; den Mitarbeiterinnen und Mitarbeitern des Hirmer Verlags für ihr Engagement; Silke Probst für ihr gewissenhaftes, kluges und umsichtiges Lektorat; Katja Kraft für ihr hilfreiches Feedback; Nick Trachte, Chef des Münchner Boxwerks, der als einer der Ersten von dieser Idee erfahren hat und das Buch, die Ausstellung und deren Begleitprogramm mit seinem Wissen und seinen Kontakten entscheidend bereichert hat; Thomas Schuhmacher, meinem Trainer, der zwar keinen Weltmeister mehr aus mir machen wird, mit dem es aber jedes Mal eine Freude ist, im Ring zu stehen; Isa und Rosalie, den Champions meines Lebens.

My thanks go to Katharina Alt, without whose fabulous photographs this book would not exist; Thomas Zuhr for his willingness to embark on this project, for his enthusiasm and his suggestions; The staff of Hirmer Verlag for their dedication; Silke Probst for her scrupulous, savvy and prudent copy-editing; Katja Kraft for her helpful feedback; Nick Trachte, manager of the Boxwerk boxing gym in Munich, who was one of the first to learn of this idea: this book, the exhibition and the program of supporting events were crucially enriched by his knowledge and his contacts; Thomas Schuhmacher, my trainer with whom it is always a joy to be in the ring, even if I am no longer World champion material; Isa and Rosalie, the champions of my life.

— Impressum | Colophon

Published by:
Hirmer Verlag
Nymphenburger Straße 84
80636 Munich, Germany

Accompanying exhibition:
Museum Fünf Kontinente, Munich
May 13 – September 11, 2016
www.museum-fuenf-kontinente.de

Editor: Michael Schleicher
Concept: Thomas Zuhr
Authors: Petra Giloy-Hirtz, Michael Schleicher, Charles Schumann, Claudia Strand

Image and artists rights:
© Abrar, Anoush & Hoving, Amiée: 7; © akg-images / Jürgen Raible: 27; © Alt, Katharina: 4, 8, 42/43, 52 –145, 174 –183; © Brettschuh, Gerald: 30/31; © Gehrke, Simon / Nick Trachte, Boxwerk: 173; © ullstein bild – AP / Mitsunori Chigita: 13; © ullstein bild – Granger, NYC: 22, 37; © ullstein bild – Philipp Kester: 21; © ullstein bild – United Archives: 14; © ullstein bild - Lebrecht Music & Arts / Eamonn McCabe: 39; © Estate of George Grosz, Princeton, N. J. / VG Bild-Kunst, Bonn 2016: 29; © Zuhr, Thomas: 152/153
In some cases it was not possible to identify the holders of the rights in the illustrations. However, legitimate claims will be compensated by the publisher in line with to the usual terms.

English translation: Bram Opstelten, Richmond
German copy editing and proof reading: Stefanie Adam, Munich
English copy editing: Philippa Hurd, London
English proof reading: Jane Michael, Munich

Hirmer project management: Rainer Arnold
Layout and typesetting: Hannes Halder
Pre-press and repro: Reproline Mediateam GmbH, Munich

Printing and Binding: Westermann Druck Zwickau
Paper: Magno Satin 150g/sqm
Printed in Germany

Bibliographic information published by the Deutsche Nationalbibliothek
The Deutsche Nationalbibliothek lists this publication in the Deutsche Nationalbibliografie; detailed bibliographic data is available on the Internet at http://www.dnb.de.

© 2016 Hirmer Verlag GmbH, Munich; Katharina Alt; the Authors.

ISBN 978-3-7774-2612-9

Follow the editor on twitter: @DerSchleicher
www.katharinaalt.de
www.hirmerverlag.de | www.hirmerpublishers.com

Kindly supported by: